The
Kentucky
Thoroughbred

D1707795

The Kentucky Thoroughbred

KENT HOLLINGSWORTH

Foreword by Edward L. Bowen

THE UNIVERSITY PRESS OF KENTUCKY

The Kentucky Thoroughbred was originally published as part of the Kentucky Bicentennial Bookshelf.

Copyright © 2009 by The University Press of Kentucky

Scholarly publisher for the Commonwealth,
serving Bellarmine University, Berea College, Centre College of Kentucky, Eastern Kentucky University, The Filson Historical Society, Georgetown College, Kentucky Historical Society, Kentucky State University, Morehead State University, Murray State University, Northern Kentucky University, Transylvania University, University of Kentucky, University of Louisville, and Western Kentucky University. All rights reserved.

Editorial and Sales Offices: The University Press of Kentucky
663 South Limestone Street, Lexington, Kentucky 40508-4008
www.kentuckypress.com

13 12 11 10 09   5 4 3 2 1

The Library of Congress has cataloged the hardcover edition as follows:

Hollingsworth, Kent.
    The Kentucky thoroughbred.
    Includes index.
    1. Thoroughbred horse—History. 2. Race horses—
Kentucky—Biography. 3. Horses—Kentucky—Breeding—
History. 4. Horses—Kentucky—Biography. I. Title.
SF293.T5H58 1985   636.1'32'09769   85–3149
ISBN-10: 0-8131-1547-7 (cloth)
ISBN-13: 978-0-8131-9189-8 (pbk. : alk. paper)

This book is printed on acid-free recycled paper meeting the requirements of the American National Standard for Permanence in Paper for Printed Library Materials.

Manufactured in the United States of America.

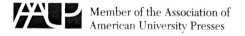

Member of the Association of American University Presses

Contents

Color illustrations follow page 78

Foreword

The Kentucky Thoroughbred was originally published in 1976 as part of what was aptly called the Kentucky Bicentennial Bookshelf. The series was prompted, of course, by the nationwide observation that two hundred years had passed since a group of determined traitors to one government got serious about creating a wondrous new one and thus began a transformation of their identity from rebels to patriots.

The importance of the Thoroughbred horse in Kentucky's economy, culture, and soul had abided through more than half of those twenty decades, and thus it was a proper subject for the University Press of Kentucky to include on its bookshelf. Selection of the author was a masterstroke, albeit one that predestined considerable hair pulling by the publisher as the deadline for completion approached, passed, was refigured, and approached again.

Kent Hollingsworth was many things, and one of them was a perfectionist. This is contradictory in a sense because he was also a pragmatist and thus understood that perfection is a goal that invariably slips over the horizon untouched. From no one did he demand more effort in that chase than from himself.

As editor and then publisher of the Thoroughbred trade magazine the *Blood-Horse*, Hollingsworth assigned himself the weekly task of commenting on the sport and industry in a one-page column, What's Going On Here. For more than two decades, Kent strove to make his column a gem of logic, importance, relevance, and style. He crusaded for what he believed was best for the sport and against any and all challenges to its integrity, tradition, prosperity, and charm.

As his managing editor, I had the task of making sure the other editorial matter of the magazine was in order, and the boss's page was generally the last to reach my desk. In the final days before weekly publication, a succession of sheets of paper were ripped from Kent's typewriter and reduced to wads in and around his wastebasket. Each version was good but, he felt, could somehow be made better—perhaps perfect. Time lingered heavily on the hands of the editorial staff awaiting the moment when Kent would pad, in his socks, from his office to ours, completed opus in hand. I was the first to read his columns and the first to marvel again and again at how high the bar was set, and remained.

Kent's compulsion for excellence went beyond his professional strivings. I once dropped by his office to see how the column was coming and was several sentences in to what was under the typewriter bar before I realized I was intruding on a personal matter. It seems one of his beloved daughters had developed, or was considering developing, some sort of connection with a fellow who by trade was a carpenter. Kent counseled that one could not generalize too readily about carpenters. One, he pointed out, had made a mistake more than a century before that meant that this very daughter's bedroom window still leaked, whereas another carpenter, he reminded her, had changed the history of humanity some two thousand years before. All around were the telltale signs of Kent's effort—the wadded and discarded versions. Even in a matter addressed to only one person, he kept at it until it was the best he could make it be.

Although such character comes from within, Kent's background provided numerous stepping-stones to his lasting success and importance as a journalist, historian, and teacher.

He was born on August 21, 1929, in St. Louis, and he treasured his baseball cap from the old St. Louis Browns. He described his father as "a civil engineer, oil producer, and Thoroughbred breeder," his mother as "a poet, playwright, and horseplayer." Raising a few horses was a sideline to Denzil Hollingsworth, whose sense of adventure was satisfied more by gambling on drilling sites. Nevertheless, Kent's father did provide the opportunity to write years later of a forlorn last-place finish in the 1946 Kentucky Derby, gamely summarized as "Well, son, we've had a Derby horse."

The Hollingsworths moved to Scott County, Kentucky, when Kent was about ten years old. Living on a farm provided him with experience in performing all manner of chores with barnyard animals. Nor was his experience with horses confined to Thoroughbreds. He proudly recalled harnessing draft horses on his tiptoes, as well as mowing fields, mucking stalls, and, later, exercising racehorses at home and working at various racetracks.

Kent graduated from old University High School, beloved as "U High" by those who remember it. He was a team manager for Adolph Rupp's high-flying University of Kentucky Wildcats basketball team, and he graduated from the university in 1950 with a degree in journalism. Kent enlisted in the army in 1952. He was of a bent that the challenges, both physical and mental, of Officer Candidate School appealed to him, and after graduation he was a tank gunnery instructor at Fort Knox. Following his release from active duty in 1954, he worked at various jobs in both advertising and reporting for the *Lexington Leader*, the *Blood-Horse*, and *Sports Illustrated*. He also attended the University of Kentucky College of Law, graduating in 1959, and for a time thereafter added legal matters related to the horse industry to his varied workload.

Along the way, Kent developed a great knowledge and appreciation of the Thoroughbred sport and business. This included a devotion to the sporting principles, without which the game would not have interested him, and a fascination for the wide range of personalities involved, who have little in common save a connection to the horse. Covering these dramatis personae put him in contact with captains of industry, hardworking horsemen, aristocrats, and others who fell into the category of "characters." Each type held some fascination for him, but he tended to let individuals earn respect rather than be granted it.

By the time he became editor of the *Blood-Horse* in 1963, he was steeped in the history and best literature of the turf, which is to say, he had read a great deal of Joseph Estes and Joe Palmer from his own era and of Walter Vosburgh and John Hervey from another. From this base, he never ceased to learn. Years later, when Alex Haley, the author of *Roots*, dropped by the *Blood-Horse* office during the height of his fame to discuss an idea he had about another novel, Kent was so conversant with early-nineteenth-century racing in the Deep South that Haley likened the visit to being in a historians' fraternity.

Kent had a deep respect for journalism and, in fact, often gave me to think he would rather have edited a great newspaper than a magazine. He was adept at instilling respect for accuracy, fairness, and thoroughness in his staff, who tended to see him both as mentor and as employer. At the same time, his manner of expression was forever fresh, sometimes challenging, and often inspiring. He embraced computers, fax machines, and other technology that changed how newsrooms looked, sounded, and were managed—that is, he embraced them on behalf of his staff. He personally clung to the familiar comfort of his typewriter.

Kent was well read and interested in many subjects. In the busiest days at the *Blood-Horse*, he was a member of a local group that called itself the Cricket Club. Each member in his turn gave a talk on a serious subject while hosting dinner. Kent never took the easy route of speaking on something he knew without diligent preparation.

His training in the law honed his thinking process and was influential the rest of his life. Kent was the intellectual equivalent of a feisty point guard on the basketball court—seeking results through great effort, cognizant of what others were doing or failing to do, impatient with laxity and compromise. Following the rules, and laws, was a given. This in part enabled him to reach far outside journalism to exert influence on horse racing. He drafted the revised Kentucky Racing Act and rewrote the state's racing rules, giving legal clout to many of his principles for the sport. When federal legislation threatened the industry, he was involved in the efforts in Washington DC that resulted in the formation of the American Horse Council to protect and foster the entire horse world. This led to a role in the crafting of the Interstate Horseracing Act, which still regulates interstate wagering, as well as a role rewriting the obsolete tax schedule for depreciation of horses. These were services not generally assigned to a journalist but for which he was uniquely qualified.

In his later years, Kent transferred his teaching abilities into the classroom proper, conducting courses on equine law at the

University of Louisville, where another generation of admirers gathered round. He passed away in 1999.

To those who might dismiss a three-decades-old history, a polite rejoinder is justified: While it is true that much has happened in Thoroughbred racing since 1976, author Kent Hollingsworth has provided a solid, entertaining, and provocative background for putting more recent happenings into context. Understanding and appreciating the circuitous routes of happenstance and design that are the history of the Kentucky Thoroughbred will enhance readers' understanding and appreciation of the scene in 2009 and beyond.

Besides, as always, Kent Hollingsworth provides a darn good read.

Edward L. Bowen

Preface

As a usual thing, a volume on a bicentennial bookshelf might be expected to contain some hard facts, neatly arranged in chronological order, calculated to provide a skeletal record of the development of a native industry over 200 years.

The Thoroughbred has a skeleton, of course, and we could rattle such dry bones as 1797, and 1 1/4 miles run in 1:59 2/5, and syndication of two stallions for $11.2 million, and we could pile economic-impact indicators on pari-mutuels data 16.2 hands high—but this would not describe the horse.

Why do you imagine 163,628 people, most of whom would admit to possessing no particular musical talent, at least as to warrant public performance, suddenly on the first Saturday in May at Churchill Downs become so emotionally involved as to accompany a high school band playing "My Old Kentucky Home"?

Why would a group of men come all the way from Japan to the Keeneland yearling sale in Kentucky and raise the $500,000 opening bid by an Irish bloodstock agent to $600,000 to obtain an unraced, unnamed, one-year-old son of Bold Ruler?

What attracts countless numbers of camera-wielding tourists to the tree-shaded pikes of Central Kentucky to peer through white plank fences at idly grazing mares and foals? More than 75,000 each year signed the visitors' register at Faraway Farm and heard old Will Harbut brighten the legend that was Man o' War: ". . . and he look over to that Whitney hoss and he say, 'Now you come on, Grier, iffin you can' . . . and a man comes here and offers a million dollars for him and Mr. Riddles says, 'No, lots of men might have a million dollahs, but only one man can have Man o' War . . . stand still, Red . . . 'cause, he wuz de mostest hoss. . . ."

The tendency of historians to attach significance to dates and to marshal the figures shall be resisted here. As calcium and phosphorous content cannot describe the beauty of a bluegrass pasture or Elkhorn Creek, so the date sixty men met in Postlethwait's Tavern in Lexington and formed the Kentucky Association for the Improvement of the Breeds of Stock or the precise amount of state tax revenue derived from pari-mutuel wagering does not explain the meaning of the Thoroughbred in Kentucky.

The intention here is to set down an account of a few good horses, and the people who concerned themselves with the raising of these horses. The stories will be largely factual, for the performances and pedigrees of Thoroughbreds are better documented, more accurately and over a longer period of time, than those for people, but readers should be forewarned that racing men do not always speak of their horses in affidavit form. In truth, much of the reputation the Kentucky Bluegrass now commands as the premier section of the world for the raising of racehorses is based on the oral testimony of nineteenth-century breeders of horses that could not run a mile in less than 1:40, but who would bet you hard cash, hard whiskey, or horse-for-horse (the winner taking the loser's horse home) that he could beat yours at catch weights.

Therefore, those who would seek a concise, 200-year chronology of the Thoroughbred industry in Kentucky are left to shift for themselves amidst the following metachronistic collage of facts and fancies that men have contributed to the broad tradition of fleetness of the Kentucky blood horse.

Acknowledgments

No ATTEMPT has been made herein to designate corroborative documentation by footnotes. As a personal matter, I abhor the harsh punctuation afforded by a superior number and in my reading have developed skill in ignoring such proffered textual interruptions. The thought here is that if a statement is so preposterous as to be unworthy of belief, a footnote indicating where it previously had been published renders it no more credible; prior publication, in itself, does not vouchsafe verity. In point of fact, virtually everything in this volume previously has appeared, one or more times in various forms, in *The Blood-Horse* magazine. Cluttering this volume with citations to earlier efforts on the same subject hardly could enhance its authority.

Still, some indication that material was not cut from whole cloth is in order when writing of matters not personally witnessed, as is the case when addressing history. A listing of primary sources is essential, if only to provide an opportunity for those so inclined to determine whether an author had any evidence for his inferences drawn and presented as historical fact. Certainly credit should be given to those scholarly researchers whose work product was reviewed, evaluated, and used in forming one's individual concept of that which must have occurred. In the course of reading and writing about a single subject over a period of years, one has a tendency to pick up notions, phrases, attitudes from earlier writers; these are assimilated, some embraced and in time adopted as one's very own. Such adverse possession is wrong. It is subliminal thievery. If one reads enough, it is called erudition.

My reading has been restricted. There are those who grew up on Dickens and Dumas, Cooper and Washington Irving, others introduced to the language by Mark Twain or Henry L. Mencken. My frame of reference is derived from Joe Estes, Joe Palmer, and John Hervey.

For thirty years, Joe Estes was *The Blood-Horse*. He was a scholar. He also was a gag writer. He was a statistician, and a poet. He was a handicapper, and a geneticist. He was a historian, and a computer programmer. He was a master of whimsy, and a deft literary infighter. He was a frail man of towering intellectual strength, recognized throughout the world as the foremost authority on matters pertaining to the Thoroughbred. His research studies overturned the Rule of Thumb in breeding, reversed and remanded it for new trials in conformance with his opinions on the probabilities as favoring the mating of horses of demonstrated high racing class, rather than horses distinguished only by pedigree.

Joe Palmer, who lectured in English literature at the University of Kentucky during his ten years as managing editor of *The Blood-Horse*, moved to New York in 1944 as turf editor for the *Herald-Tribune* and CBS, yet continued to brighten *The Blood-Horse* with his weekly column until his death in 1952. Earlier on, he wrote of horses, *Names in Pedigrees*, but he was interested more in racing men than their horses, confessing to be "no noted lover of the horse, but a way of life of which the horse was once, and in a few favored places still is, a symbol—a way of charm and ease and grace and leisure. Grace and charm should perhaps not be tampered with at this late date but, at whatever risk of boasting, I am as good at ease and leisure as any man alive."

John Hervey compiled the definitive history of the early Thoroughbred here, *Racing in America;* volumes 1 and 2 covered the two centuries from 1665 to 1865, the importation of Bulle Rock in 1730 up to the Civil War. Walter Vosburgh's earlier volume in this invaluable series published by The Jockey Club covered racing in America from the Civil War through 1921. Hervey in volume 4 covered the period from 1922 through 1936. Hervey's comprehensive research touched all the usual original sources and more; his collection of stallion broadsides, family letters, diaries, and rare issues of eighteenth- and nineteenth-century newspapers and sporting journals, from which he drew much of his data, unfortunately was dispersed upon his death.

Primary sources for Estes, Palmer, Hervey, and all writers of the history of the Thoroughbred in America are contemporary race summaries as appear in the *American Turf Register, Spirit of the Times*, Krik's and Goodwin's *Guides to the Turf*, and *Daily Racing Form* chart books, whose race reports, errors and all, have been accepted as true.

Special acknowledgment should be given to the late John L. O'Connor, who during the 1920s turned every page of Lexington's oldest newspapers and transcribed everything therein pertaining to Thoroughbreds, including advertisements, compiling a rare volume privately printed by Louis Lee Haggin and entitled *Notes on the Thoroughbred from Kentucky Newspapers*.

I also relied on Lewis Collins's 1847 *History of Kentucky;* George W. R. Ranck's 1872 *History of Lexington, Kentucky;* Benjamin G. Bruce's chapter on the Thoroughbred written in 1882 for Dr. Robert Peter's *History of Fayette County;* Lyman Weeks's 1898 *The American Turf;* C. R. Staples's 1939 *The History of Pioneer Lexington, 1781–1806;* and Dan Bowmar III's articles in *The Blood-Horse* reprinted in 1960 as *Giants of the Turf*.

To these stark branches, I add the flower of Colonel Phil T. Chinn's taped recollections. In 1954 I spent a summer of evenings with a recorder listening to Colonel Chinn's stories. While these recollections may have digressed from generally accepted historical fact in some instances, the thought remains that if one really wishes to gain some idea of racing men and how the game was played in an earlier day, he had best send a car around for the colonel.

SARAZEN

COLONEL PHIL T. CHINN was the real article, a Kentucky Colonel in appearance, manner, and business profession, a player and layer in the game of racing for nearly eighty-eight years. He had a courtliness which charmed Lillian Russell, entranced customers of yearlings, awed creditors, and enthralled casual acquaintances.

His father was Black Jack Chinn, noted in the legend and fact of Kentucky history as a prominent politician, race starter, co-owner of Kentucky Derby winner Leonatus, and chairman of the first Kentucky racing commission.

Young Chinn was at old Washington Park when Snapper Garrison delayed the start of a race for more than an hour, then won the 1893 American Derby with Boundless. He was the leading owner and trainer at the old Santa Anita meetings of 1905–1906. He was at Juarez when Pancho Villa's lieutenant called a meeting of Colonel Matt Winn's racing officials, jammed a knife in the conference table, and announced there would be no race meeting until Colonel Phil T. Chinn was reinstated—which was done forthwith. He was at Charleston when a storm blew down the betting-ring tent and one of Chicago O'Brien's biggest parlays went with the wind.

In the 1920s, Colonel Chinn was America's most spectacular horse seller. After disposing of nearly a hundred

1

yearlings at Saratoga, he would return to Lexington and sell another fifty at the old Kentucky Association track. For eleven years, his Saratoga consignments sold for more than double that of the market average. He sold Hustle On for $70,000 in 1927 at Saratoga; he sold Airmans Guide for $7,500 at Keeneland in 1958. He pinhooked good-looking youngsters, and breeders sought him out in the hope that he would present their yearlings in the Chinn consignment.

"Hiram Steele, whom I respected very much, had quit John E. Madden and returned to Dr. Marius Johnston's place," Colonel Chinn recalled. "Hiram kept after me to come out and see two yearlings—said Madden, Kay Spence, B. B. and Montfort Jones had been looking at them. Well I thought then they couldn't be much horses or they would have been sold, so I stalled him around.

"Finally, I came face to face with Hiram in the Phoenix Hotel and I thought, here it goes, I can't stall this man any further, I'll have to finish this deal right now. I said, 'Hiram, I've been looking for you. On my way out to your place to see those yearlings at this moment and I would be very pleased if you could accompany me.'

"Well, we rode out there in a buggy and just as we were pulling into the yard I said, 'Hiram, we've talked about everything—women, politics, who made the best whiskey in Kentucky—but let us get down to the business at hand. What are these yearlings by?'

"He then said something about High Time. 'That settles it. I wouldn't want to disappoint you or Dr. Johnston for the world, so I'll look at them, but I don't imagine you could chloroform me and get me to pay more than a dollar and a half apiece for them.'"

The yearlings were in the first crop by High Time, which Colonel Chinn had trained three years earlier. Intensely inbred, High Time was out of a Domino mare and was by Ultimus, he by a Domino sire out of a Domino mare. As a two-year-old in 1918, High Time had raced six

2

times and won once, setting a track record for five furlongs in the Hudson Stakes.

"He was a bleeder, though, quit faster than he commenced," said Colonel Chinn. "I was not cognizant of this, however, when Mr. Sam Ross invited me to train him. Although not altogether familiar with the colt, I understood he had won a stakes and I felt that would make him eligible for the Chinn stable, so I said I would be very pleased indeed to train him. I soon found out he was a bleeder, but at that time I was confident I had an adequate remedy for such a situation.

"Before long, I had him working marvelously; he was breaking all world records, the short distances he went. I thought he could fall down, jump over two barrels and crawl the last quarter to win, and I so advised Mr. Ross and his associate in this matter, Admiral Cary Grayson. I had quite some change at the time and I bet pretty fair—that was when I acquired a bad impression of this horse.

"It was at Saratoga. He went right out there on the lead, run the first half in :47 and something; but it took him about :35 to get the last quarter. He was beaten fifteen lengths. Mr. Ross and Admiral Grayson came by the barn after the heat and acknowledged the horse had not run well, a point on which I agreed. I said I felt terrible about it, but I informed them I knew how they could make $1,400 on the horse: 'Gentlemen, I want you to know I have the warmest feeling for you personally, but if you can get that horse out of my barn by sundown, you may forget my $1,400 training bill.'

"So I said to Hiram, 'If I had known these two colts were by High Time, I don't believe I would have been too enthusiastic about seeing them.' But by that time we had arrived at the barn and he opened the stall door. There was Time Exposure—well, he was only five pounds back of Sarazen at two—a marvelous race horse.

"I said, 'Well, so he's by High Time. But he must have

breeding on the dam's side.' Hiram said no, the colt was out of a mare that had been plowing down there in the garden. And the other colt was out of a mare Dr. Johnston gave $37.50 for, 'but he's the best horse we've ever raised here.' I asked to see the other one and Hiram was right; he was the best-looking horse I had ever seen—the perfect horse. That was Sarazen.

"Of course, these were two real horses. There was no horse better than Sarazen during his period. Of those he met, he beat them all, mud or dry, cyclone or volcano, beat them at the gate and beat them under the wire."

Colonel Chinn bought the pair for $2,500. Time Exposure was to win twenty-two races, including the Tijuana Thanksgiving Handicap. The colonel sold him as a two-year-old to Frank Farrell for $15,000. Sarazen was unbeaten in ten starts as a two-year-old.

"In his first start, I got a good, hoop-de-doo rider, an Indian named Martinez who was recommended as not one to pull a horse that was carrying a little change. You know, there was a certain kind of rider in those days who would pull a horse on you when a great deal of money was down.

"So I told Martinez, 'I'll give some consideration over and above the normal fare upon the condition you do not hit this horse, just kick him once or twice to get him away and don't win by more than a length.' Well, the boy couldn't hold him, opened up by five, won by two or three lengths.

"So I got Mack Garner to ride him next time; he's on top by four before the others leave the barrier, wins by eight lengths, pretty near tied the Hawthorne track record that day, you know; just a helluva horse. Then I took him to Saratoga, won by four, and made a sucker play—sold the horse to Mrs. Graham Fair Vanderbilt for $30,000 and he was worth $100,000."

Trained by Max Hirsch, Sarazen won the Champagne, Oakdale, National, Laurel Special, and Pimlico Serial against older horses as a two-year-old. Champion at three,

4

he won the Carter, Fleetwing, Saranac, Huron, Manhattan, Arverne, and Maryland handicaps, and the International Special Number 3 defeating Epinard, Chilhowee, Princess Doreen, Chacolet, My Play, Mad Play, and Altawood. Time for Sarazen's first race at ten furlongs was 2:00 4/5, almost two seconds under the Latonia record and the fastest 1 1/4 miles up to that time, with the exception of the oft-disputed two-minute Suburban of 1913 won by Whisk Broom II.

"You know, the morning I bought those two yearlings from Dr. Johnston, I caught the first train to Washington to see Admiral Grayson. Said I was in a mind to do a little horse trading and he says with what. 'Kinda like to try that old High Time again, as a stud.' We talked around there for a while and he finally gave me half of High Time for nothing. As you know, he turned out to be a terrific stallion."

Under Colonel Chinn's management, High Time led the general sire list in 1929, the same year he also was leading sire of two-year-olds in winners and money earned. At one time Colonel Chinn refused an offer of $150,000, then a record sum for a stallion.

"Admiral Grayson wrote me one day that he had received an offer to sell his half-interest in High Time and that I could match it or he would sell to the man and the horse would be moved to Virginia. I told him there would be some difficulty about removing my half of the horse to Virginia, but that to avoid any unpleasantness I would pay $50,000 for Admiral Grayson's half. I asked him when he would be desirous of payment and he said there need be no hurry—three weeks or thirty days.

"Recovering from this shock—I had no walking around money at the time—I went over to the telegraph office and addressed the following communication to my longtime friend, W. H. (Fatty) Anderson: 'If no inconvenience to you, I would appreciate your sending $35,000 to Lexington by Monday, at which time I will have secured the remaining necessaries from my bank. Yours truly.'

"Upon the appointed day I inquired of my secretary if by chance we had received any communication from California, and she informed me that $50,000 was on hand, together with a wire that said, 'Any man who can use 35 can use 50. Regards.'

"Fatty was a man of some sophistication."

One of the reasons Colonel Chinn happened to think of Anderson was that he had sold him a nice horse only a few years earlier. That was Carlaris, which won seven of his first eight races for Anderson early in 1926, including the Tijuana Derby by seven lengths, reducing the track record by two seconds, and the rich Coffroth Handicap by eight lengths, reducing the track standard by 1 1/5 seconds. This reminded the colonel of the part Carlaris played in the brief racing venture near Ashland, Kentucky, a track named Raceland which opened with a flourish in 1924 and closed with a shudder in a 1928 bankruptcy proceeding.

"Tom Cromwell, Jack Keene, and I were having dinner one night at the Lafayette Hotel in Lexington and in a casual way I introduced a suggestion that we build a race track to go in opposition to Polk Laffoon. At the time, Laffoon about owned Covington; he had the power company, the transit company, the gas company, the bridge, some banks, was president of the Latonia track and vice chairman of the racing commission.

"They asked where we would set up this operation. I said I didn't much care—Bowling Green, Paducah, Ashland. Well, one day we went over to Ashland and after I looked over the layout I weakened. So did Cromwell. But Keene was a great builder.

"Cromwell and I laid back, let Keene have his head and sort of walked over the ground. Cromwell said he wasn't too game about going into the thing and I said I wasn't an enthusiastic man about losing money. This man we had, J. O. Keene, while one of the finest men in the world—there was no more chance of limiting him to $250,000

Colonel Phil T. Chinn
(*Keeneland-Cook*)

W. H. (Fatty) Anderson

Admiral Cary Grayson
(*Keeneland-Cook*)

than of holding John D. Rockefeller to a dime's worth of gasoline.

"We had some intimate discussions with Jack on the matter and he finally convinced us $250,000 would be enough, so we said go ahead. It was called the Tri-State Fair and Racing Association and Charley Berryman was president, a local man named Williamson was vice president, Keene was general manager, Cromwell secretary, handicapper, steward, and other things, and John S. Barbee was treasurer.

"Well, it wasn't long before Keene had spent $300,000 for the finest stables in the land, but he had no grandstand or track. We needed more money. Berryman had exhausted his people. There was only one man who could raise any more money—P. T. Chinn. So I went to New York and got $100,000 from Elmer Smathers. That was spent before I returned, necessitating a trip to Chicago. Charles B. Shaffer sprang for another $200,000 . . . finest sportsman in the world . . . he said at the time the track would never go. 'You have one of the finest plants I have ever seen. Only one thing wrong with it, it's in the wrong place. Should be in New York.'

"You know, the day before the track was to open, it was not completed. Keene had the stretch in the wrong place, 'way over to the left instead of down in front of the stands. So I said to Jack, 'Where are your blueprints? Let me see the blueprints of this track.'

"He didn't even look at me, said, 'I don't use blueprints; I build by eye.'

"Actually, the track never really got started. They held a couple of meetings, but from the onset there was financial stress, and then one day—I believe it was Black Maria's year—Charley Berryman came to me and suggested it would be a great personal favor if I would be kind enough to ship my stable to Raceland.

"Seeing no way out of the situation, I agreed that I would. The purses there were not in keeping with my needs, but I figured I might be able to make the mutuels pay the freight inasmuch as I had a considerable number of maidens only one man knew anything about—namely, P. T. Chinn.

"I conned Fatty Anderson to go with me. He had the best horse in the country at the time, unbeatable in the West, but he was not too keen about going to Ashland. I told him it was the greatest place in the world to summer his horses, and in addition there were places to dine unrivaled this side of the Atlantic. I described the mountainous servings of fried chicken, accompanied by diverse delicacies—I knew nothing about the place, really—and Anderson finally agreed to ship in.

"Well, we went over there for opening day, the entries came out, and he said what about it? I replied that it appeared I would win three races out of my stable and he decided there was only one thing to do.

"He took a night train to Cincinnati, arranged with Louis Katz to obtain the best possible price on all three horses with all the money he could get on, and returned at 9 o'clock the following morning.

"I saw him early in the day and he appeared haggard—quite possibly the railroad from Ironton was the roughest railroad in the world—but he said he was going to bet all the money he had on him through the machines on other horses in the races to build up the odds on my horses, and that I was in for half on the Cincinnati deal."

On July 5, opening day of the 1926 meeting at Raceland, Colonel Chinn ran three horses.

The second race was won by P. T. Chinn's two-year-old maiden filly, Muriel H., by Rock View, trained by C. E. Patterson and ridden by Graceton Philpot, paying $3.60 for $2.

The fifth race, the $2,000-added Ashland Handicap, was won by W. C. Baxter's Malcolm B. Jr., by Torchbearer, bred by Colonel Chinn, trained by Patterson, and ridden by Philpot, paying $3. He won by two lengths, setting a track record for seven furlongs.

"I had sold that horse to Baxter, but kept him in my

9

stable because I more or less managed all his racing interests. After Malcolm B. Jr. won, Anderson came up to me and said, 'You know how much money we've won so far?' I had no idea, but I figured it would not be much because nobody would handle a good sum on opening day at a small track—fifty thousand? 'I'm not talking about pocket change,' Anderson says. 'We've got an unlimited bet on and the clocker tells me he can't find a work on this third horse you're running. Not one! And we've got everything going back on him!'

"I said, 'Anderson, I'm deeply sorry about that, but it is too late to work him. The horse is going on the track at this moment.' "

The sixth race was won by P. T. Chinn's Hot Time, by High Time, which Philpot eased home by six lengths. He paid $8.80 for $2.

"So I saw Fatty and suggested that we take in one of those chicken places about eight miles down the road, and he said, 'That's the idea, let's get some of that chicken, corn-on-the-cob, radishes—eat this big day off.'

"It just so happened a flash flood came up just as we arrived. No chicken. We got back to Ashland about 11 o'clock and, of course, all the eateries were closed. We went back to the hotel and had some beer.

"It was terribly hot, and virtually impossible to sleep, but we finally settled down. We were staying in Ironton, you know, and about 3 o'clock in the morning Henry Ford's coal train came out of one of those mountains with what must have been 200 cars going a mile a minute right under our window.

"Wake a man in the horse business and you'll never get him back to sleep. Anderson decided it was time for him to depart. He dressed, went downstairs, ordered his car, and was then informed by the attendant that the fellow who had borrowed the car for the evening had not returned. About that time, the night clerk handed Anderson a wire.

10

"Anderson turns to me and he says, 'Phil, this certainly is a delightful place and I have enjoyed myself. That was a lovely dinner last night; the train, I can assure you, has left town; my car has been stolen, and now I learn that the three races we won were to no avail inasmuch we did not get five cents down on them. I imagine about the only way you could attract me to Raceland again would be with a hog chain.'

"As you can understand, I felt somewhat derelict as host in this situation, but I believed our friendship would not be altered appreciably if Carlaris brought off the Raceland Derby—and I was as sure of that as Citation in a $1,500 claiming race.

"I had Malcolm B. Jr. in the Derby and Strother Griffin was to ride him. The morning of the race I went out on the track with a pony and I said: 'Strother, I know you'd like to win the Derby, but you haven't got a 1–1,000 chance of beating Carlaris, so don't punish our horse, just get him off good and let him run; there isn't a horse in the country can beat Carlaris right now.'

"Anderson called me later that day, said he had $50,000 on Carlaris and was declaring me in for $5,000, which was stretching me pretty well. Anderson thought no more of betting $100,000 than I would about smoking a Corona-Corona.

"They had a band follow the horses to the post, cymbals clanging and all that. Carlaris was a nervous horse under normal conditions, but he was finished that day before the race was run. He broke on top by fifteen lengths after a quarter-mile was run, was ten lengths on top going into the backstretch, then collapsed over at the three-eighths pole.

"Strother rode a perfect race on Malcolm B. Jr. Won by a length going away. Well, I never felt so bad in my life. Here I had just dropped $5,000 and lovely people were all around me, congratulating me, patting me on the back, and somebody put a wreath of roses around my neck. I thought I was going to choke to death."

LEXINGTON

Kentucky's association with the Thoroughbred antedates its admission as a state, even its settlement, though the connection is admittedly tenuous. In 1750 the Loyal Land Company was formed at Charlottesville, Virginia, and secured a grant of 800,000 acres in the "district of Kentucke." To get a line on what it had, the company sent out an exploring party headed by Dr. Thomas Walker, who found a gap through the mountains and a river which took his party farther into the wilderness beyond. He named all three—the gap, mountains, and river—after the Duke of Cumberland, son of King George II, who as commander-in-chief of the British army had gained some military renown, and the lasting hatred of the Scots, at Culloden. The royal duke's defeat by the French at Hastenbeck in 1757 ended his military career, however, and thereafter he devoted himself to horseracing and gambling as a founding member of the English Jockey Club, and to his stud at Windsor. An unattractive man, whose vices and defects may have been magnified by the Scots, he died of obesity at the age of forty-four, the year Eclipse was foaled. Whatever his military and social shortcomings were, no man ever was to exert such profound or lasting influence on the Thoroughbred breed as did the Duke of Cumberland: He bred two of the three foundation sires, both Herod and Eclipse.

All Thoroughbreds today descend directly in tail-male line from three eighteenth-century English stallions. The tail-male line of a horse's pedigree is the paternal line, traceable in human genealogy by following the surname from father to grandfather and back to its originator. Tracing the tail-male line in any Thoroughbred pedigree today, one invariably encounters one of the three foundation sires: Matchem, foaled in 1748; Herod, foaled in 1758; and Eclipse, foaled in 1764, unbeaten on the race course and forebear in direct male line of about 90 percent of today's Thoroughbreds.

On his 1769 hunting trip to the Bluegrass region, Daniel Boone brought some horses with him through the Cumberland Gap. Indians promptly made off with these horses, and there is no evidence that they were other than pack animals anyway.

Kentucky as a whole is not really the earthly paradise Boone's description promised. The paradise is a relatively small, central portion of the state, an area of some 2,800 square miles within a thirty-mile radius of Lexington, which has become world-famous as the birthplace of blood horses. The land is fertile, with a rare outcropping of the deep Ordovician limestone, at the apex of what geologists call the Cincinnati anticline. It is rich in calcium and phosphorous, inherited from millions of shells and skeletons deposited centuries earlier when Central Kentucky was an ocean bed. It is gently rolling land and the porous nature of its subsoil assured adequate drainage, to the exclusion of marshy, soggy lands. *Poa pratensis,* today's Kentucky strain of bluegrass, was not native to the region; it is not certain when the woods and canebrakes were cleared to become bluegrass pastures, but early on the area became known as the "Yorkshire of America," which in all honesty lends greater compliment to the celebrated fertile region of England than to the Bluegrass section of Kentucky.

Early settlers came from the East either by boat down the Ohio River to what now is Maysville, or by land through the Cumberland Gap and over the Wilderness Trail. They walked or they rode horses, for the Wilderness Trail was not made suitable for wagons until 1795, and there was a considerable number of horses in the Lexington area prior to then. The Fayette County tax rolls for 1789 accounted for 9,607 horses, 56 stallions, 2,522 slaves, and nine taverns.

These were not Thoroughbreds, but they were raced, for the character of the people who came to be called Kentuckians, second sons from Virginia and Carolina seeking adventure, action, fortune in free lands, was such that when there were no Indians to chase and no stumps to be cleared, there were arguments to be settled; in Kentucky, arguments usually were settled by a horse race.

Court records show that in 1783 there were horse races at Humble's race paths and Haggin's race paths outside Harrodsburg. For betting a mare worth £12, Hugh McGary was tried at Oyer and Terminer court in August 1783 and found guilty: "The opinion of the court is that the said H. McGary, gentleman, be deemed an infamous gambler, and that he shall not be eligible to any office of trust or honor within this state—pursuant to an act of assembly entitled An act to suppress excessive gaming."

Lexington received its name in 1775, its town charter in 1782. Its first store was opened in 1784, and in 1787 John Bradford started the first newspaper west of the Alleghenies, the *Kentucke Gazette,* in which the documentation of Kentucky racehorse pedigrees began in the February 16, 1788, issue when John Davenport advertised, "The famous horse PILGARLICK of a beautiful chestnut colour, full fourteen hands three inches high, rising ten years old, will stand the ensuing season on the head of Salt River. . . . Pilgarlick was got by the noted imported horse, Janus, his dam by Silver-eye, and is the swiftest in the district of Kentucke from one to six hundred yards, Darius only excepted." Pilgarlick's acknowledged superior, Darius, was advertised the following month as to be let to mares at fifteen shillings the leap, or three pounds to insure, his pedigree being shown as "bred by Mr. Daniel Hardaway of Amelia County, Virginia, and was got by the noted imported horse Janus, his dam and grandam by the same; his great grandam by the imported horse Spanker. N.B.—Darius will be for sale after the 2nd Thursday in September, at which time there is a race depending on him."

These usually were quarter-mile dash races on straight paths or town thoroughfares, if the stumps had been cleared, a problem that confronted Lexington's Town Trustees who on March 7, 1788, "Resolved—that all streets be opened and cleared of stumps by August 1st." This in turn produced what became something of a nuisance by October 1793, and the solons approached it cautiously: "The Trustees of the town of Lexington, feeling the dangers and inconveniences which are occasioned by the practice, but too common, of racing through the streets of the in and out lotts of the town, and convinced that they are not invested with sufficient authority to put a stop to such practices, recommend it to the people of the town, to call a public meeting, to consider of the means which ought to be adopted for applying a remedy to the growing evil." The resulting election empowered the trustees to halt the custom of "jockeys racing their horses through the streets" by restricting them to the Commons, on a half-mile race path extending northwesterly along the town branch of Elkhorn Creek, from what is now Ayers Alley and Vine Street.

Precisely when distance racing came into vogue, or what field around which it was conducted, is not known, but the first advertisement of something approaching a formal race meeting appeared in the *Kentucke Gazette* of August 22, 1789:

A purse race at Lexington on the 2d Thursday in October next, free for any horse, mare or gelding, weight for age, agreeable to

15

the rules of New Market (three mile heats) the best two in three; one quarter of an hour allowed between heats for rubbing. Each subscriber to pay one guinea, and every person that enters a horse to pay two guineas including his subscription. One guinea for every horse starting to be considered as entrance money for the second best horse.

Judges to be appointed by a majority of the starters on the day of running. The horses to be entered the day before running with Mr. John Fowler, who will attend at Mr. Collins' tavern on that day. The age of the horses to be ascertained to the satisfaction of the judges appointed before they can be admitted to start, even although they have paid the entrance money &c., and the money paid remain for the good of the purse. But the starter may be admitted to start his horse at the age adjudged by the judges, agreeable to the rules of New Market. The horses to start precisely at one o'clock: Any horse not starting agreeable to the appointment, to be adjudged a distanced horse. All disputes arising to be left to the decision of the judges. Subscriptions taken in by Nicholas Lafon, Lexington.

Lexington at the time was still a cluster of log buildings; the free white male population for all Fayette County totaled 3,517 in 1791, yet annual three-day race meetings over the "Lexington Course" already had become an October custom. Similar race meetings were announced in the *Kentucke Gazette* during the 1790s to be conducted at Georgetown, Danville, Versailles, Bardstown, and Shelbyville.

In 1797 horsemen met at John Postlethwait's Tavern in Lexington and formed the first Kentucky Jockey Club, which promulgated rules that were adhered to by other Kentucky race meetings. Henry Clay was a member of this Jockey Club which conducted annual fall meetings at a circular course laid out on West Main Street in Lees Woods, on the site of the present Lexington Cemetery, "one time around the course shall be considered a mile."

The shift from impromptu quarter-mile dash races to scheduled four-mile heat races required an upgrading of racing stock. The blooded horse came from England, via Virginia. The first English stallion to be advertised in the Bluegrass was Benjamin Wharton's Blaze, a son of the Duke of Ancaster's Vandal and a mare by Holme's Young Trunnion, foaled in 1786, imported to Virginia in 1793, and announced to stand at Colonel Robert Sanders's farm near Georgetown in 1797. Blaze was the first of many English Thoroughbreds brought to Kentucky around 1800 which provided the foundation for what would evolve as the Kentucky racehorse. Among the problems that always has accompanied the standing of stallions is the collection of stud fees:

Give notice to gentlemen who are customers of my horse Blaze and those who wish to breed from him, that I mean to move him from this state next season unless they will come forward and enter their mares to the amount of 150 at five pounds, payable on note at Christmas in whiskey delivered at Lexington at market price, or note for 12 dollars for the season, or seven dollars the single leap, paid Christmas.

I find money very scarce and difficult to collect in the season and I wish to move him. The indulgence I have given has caused me to suffer much for money.—Benj. Wharton.

Date of the announcement, 1810; the message, timeless.

Notices of race meetings appeared in the Lexington paper during the first decade of the nineteenth century indicating racing, in addition to regular fall meetings at Lexington, at Maysville, Winchester, Paris, Versailles, Flemingsburg, Harrodsburg, and Richmond. Most of these were conducted under the racing rules of the Kentucky Jockey Club, but not all. For example, Bennett Young provides documentation in the *History of Jessamine County, Kentucky* (pp. 12–13), of an open race held in 1802 near Nicholasville under local rules which was won by a bull of extraordinary racing ability:

17

Major Netherland always retained his old-time dress. He wore a cut-a-way coat, short breeches with knee buckles, and low shoes with silk lacers and silver buckles. His pants were always fastened with red bands, and his long queue was tied with red ribbon. From his entrance into Nicholasville early in 1791, for 40 years he was prominent as a leader in all its affairs. He was postmaster for about 23 years and always dispensed the village hospitality with a lavish hand. Every man who had fought in the Revolutionary War or in the Indian wars either in Kentucky or in the Northwest, was his friend, and none ever went from his door hungry or uncared for.

Major Netherland had a great fondness for race horses and he not only ran his own horses, but went to see everybody else's horses who ran in the neighborhood. He owned a very fast horse for those days, which he called by the name of Fearnought. He had secured this horse in Virginia and brought him across the mountains. The horse had been trained in Virginia and made his first race at Fredericksburg in 1805, beating General Tracy's horse, Indian, in three four-mile heats. . . . Major Netherland was a fair and just man in his dealings with his fellow men. He was not averse to a good time, as people call it, and was always, even toward the end of his life, considered "one of the boys." He opened a race track on the Willoughby place near Sulphur Well, and maintained it for many years.

In 1802, there was a quarter-mile race on the track, and in the hearing of the crowd, Major Netherland announced that on a certain day (naming it) there would be another race for a purse of $50, one-mile heats, which was "free for anything with four legs and hair on."

At that time there was working on a farm a young man named Michael Arnspiger who had broken a bull to the saddle, which he rode to the mill. He immediately put the bull in training and for several days gave him turns around the race track. He used spurs on the bull and when these dug into his sides, he was accustomed to bellow.

On the day of the race, Arnspiger appeared on the ground with his bull. He had placed a dried hide of an ox on the bull's rump, and he carried a tin horn in his hands. He demanded of the judges the right to enter his animal, to which the owners of the horses vehemently objected, but Arnspiger answered by appealing to Major Netherland if he had not said that the race was free to "anything with four legs and hair on." Major Netherland admitted that he had, and explained that the bull had a right to enter.

When the drum was tapped, Arnspiger blew his horn, planted his spurs in the sides of the bull, which bounded off with a dreadful bellow, with the ox-hide flapping on his sides, and presenting a spectacle, combined with the noise, that had never been seen on the race track before. The horses immediately flew the track, and Arnspiger galloped home a winner.

The losers contended that they were swindled out of their money, that Arnspiger should not have been allowed to blow the tin horn, or use the ox-hide, and that but for this, he could not have won the race. Thereupon Arnspiger offered to take the ox-hide off and leave his tin horn at the stand, and run them from end to end.

Mr. Willoughby and Major Netherland were judges at the next start. Arnspiger again planted his spurs into the sides of the bull with redoubled fury. The loud bellow that followed drove the horses from the track again, despite the exertions of the riders, and Arnspiger pulled in the second $50 purse. With the money thus obtained, he purchased a black-smithing outfit, working for many years at his trade near Wilmore, and died there in the 1860s, in the 85th year of his age.

Readers may wonder at this point about the titled subject of this chapter. Indulgence is asked, for a champion racehorse which was to become America's leading sire for a record sixteen years, and his breeder, known as the Father of the Kentucky Turf, cannot be introduced briefly.

In 1809 Kentucky's first Jockey Club was reorganized, or supplanted, by the formation of the Lexington Jockey Club, with John L. Martin as secretary. Among the new racing rules adopted was one that required that "horses must be entered by names with the Secretary of the Club before 9 o'clock of evening preceding the day for which they are entered, or pay double at the poles, the riders are to be dressed in silk or satin jackets and to wear caps."

A subscribing member of the Lexington Jockey Club,

who duly registered his racing silks of "light blue cap, white jacket," was twenty-eight-year-old Dr. Elisha Warfield. His father had moved his family from Maryland to Lexington in 1790 and opened a general store on Main Street, soon becoming one of the town's wealthiest merchants. Young Warfield became an honor student at Transylvania University, first seat of higher education west of the Allegheny Mountains, gained a degree in medicine and became a leading practitioner in Lexington, and later returned to Transylvania University as professor of surgery and obstetrics.

Records show Dr. Warfield as owning a starter at the Lexington fall meeting of 1805. In the March 26, 1806, issue of the *Kentucky Gazette*, Dr. Warfield advertised "The Full Blooded English Race Horse TUP will stand this season at my stable in Lexington just at the back of Mr. Hunt's duck factory, where he will cover mares at $22." There followed a lengthy itemization of articles that would be accepted in lieu of cash, together with an affidavit from James Weatherby, keeper of the English *General Stud Book* and *Racing Calendar*, authoritatively vouching for Tup's particulars in pedigree and racing performances, as well as those of his sire and dam.

A stallion with a bona fide pedigree registered in the English *General Stud Book* was a rarity in Kentucky at the time and warranted considerable advertising space. Most of the Kentucky racehorses at this time were "cold blooded" horses; Kentuckians generally were more concerned with how fast a horse could race than with its pedigree. It was not until 1868 that Colonel Sanders D. Bruce compiled the first volume of his *American Stud Book*, which was a list of pedigrees that had been published in earlier periodicals from time to time. Not until 1894, when the American Jockey Club purchased the rights to the first six volumes of Bruce's *American Stud Book* and thereafter became the registrar for Thoroughbreds, did the breed really assume a degree of authenticity.

Prior to the publication of the *American Stud Book,* pedigrees of American racehorses could be written pretty much as sellers would like for them to read. There is a suspicion that the sale of a handsome colt of hybrid vigor would not fail for want of accompanying fashionable bloodlines. The accuracy or authenticity of all nineteenth-century pedigrees was directly proportionate to the knowledge and integrity of the breeder.

For the first half of the nineteenth century, Dr. Warfield was the man to whom horsemen turned as final adjudicator when a pedigree was in dispute or an interpretation of racing rules was needed. His library contained the first complete set of English *General Stud Books* and *Racing Calendars* brought across the mountains as well as files of the *American Turf Register* and the *Spirit of the Times.* Dr. Warfield's library, memory, and reputation for integrity were such that his pronouncements on racing matters were unquestioned.

To show how times have changed: In 1821 Dr. Warfield gave up the practice of medicine to make some money; he managed the many commercial interests that grew out of the Main Street store started by his father, hemp, banking, real estate, and soon became one of the wealthiest men in the state, but his primary interest apparently was breeding and racing horses.

When the Kentucky Association for the Improvement of the Breeds of Stock was formed at the Phoenix Hotel in 1826, Dr. Warfield's name was the second listed among the sixty charter members who comprised the leading Kentucky turfmen of the day. The Kentucky Association conducted its 1826 and 1827 race meetings at what was called the Old Williams Track in Lee's Woods off West Main Street while a new course was being constructed in the northeast section of Lexington at what now is Fifth and Race streets. Dr. Warfield was one of three trustees named to select the site and take title to the property on behalf of the Kentucky Association. The course originally was designed for classic racing, measuring "four miles,

21

wanting 22 yards, and rather a slow course to run over, having two sharp hills," according to a report in the November 1829 issue of the *American Turf Register*. Most of the race courses in Kentucky at the time were mile ovals; the same issue reported that the Georgetown course, nestled in a horseshoe bend of North Elkhorn Creek just north of town, was "fifty yards short of a mile, but the judges generally start the horses back, so as to make the full mile." At this late date, it is not certain whether that "generally" was an editorial comment on the laxity of Georgetown racing officials or an indication that some races actually were scheduled at distances other than a full mile.

The Union Course, opened on Long Island in 1821 not far from the present site of Aqueduct, was the first course in America to be plowed and harrowed, producing faster race times than realized over grass courses, and to be enclosed by a fence. ("Race track" is an American term, originating with the turning of the sod and pertaining to racing sites with a skinned, dirt-racing surface; grass courses the world over still are called "race courses.") The Kentucky Association course, which was opened in 1828, apparently was remodeled in 1832 to become America's second enclosed race track, with a skinned surface of about a mile; when its last race meeting was conducted in 1933, the Kentucky Association track was the oldest in America. It now is the site of a federal housing project; the gate posts and historic race fixtures, such as the Phoenix Hotel, Ashland, and Blue Grass stakes, were transferred to Keeneland.

Dr. Warfield liked the spot he picked for the Kentucky Association track. In 1827 he bought 123 adjacent acres and there built a mansion, The Meadows, from which he could view the races. His farm grew to 600 acres (fronting on the present Loudon Avenue and extending from Broadway to the Winchester Pike), and there he was to breed a succession of high-class racehorses, the culmination of which was mighty Lexington.

Dr. Elisha Warfield, Father of the Kentucky Turf
From a painting by George Peter Alexander Healy
(Photograph by Clyde T. Burke)

Lexington has been described as a triumph of breeding, which is often the case after a horse has proved to be of merit. He was by Boston, champion four-mile horse, but which did not become America's leading stallion until after Lexington was conceived. He was out of Alice Carneal, which won only once in three seasons of campaigning; Dr. Warfield declared Alice Carneal the best mare he ever bred, again in retrospect, for she produced twelve foals, half of which were top class: Lexington; Lavender, dam of Helmbold and Baden-Baden; Maid of Orleans, which won twenty-two races; Annette, which won the Brighton Plate in England and produced two stakes winners; Umpire, which won thirteen stakes in England; and Waxy, a gelding which won at two-mile heats in record time.

On March 17, 1850, Dr. Warfield was advised that Alice Carneal had dropped a colt by Boston. Dr. Warfield went out to the barn and found a strapping bay with a blaze face and four white stockings. "He looks just like John Sartorius's painting of the Darley Arabian," Dr. Warfield is said to have observed. "We'll call this colt Darley." With all due respect to Dr. Warfield's memory, Sartorius's painting of the Darley Arabian shows a bay with only three white feet.

Darley did not race at two. Dr. Warfield was seventy-two at the time and his physician and wife had ruled him off the Turf. He leased the colt's racing qualities to trainer Henry Brown, then known as Burbridge's Harry. No black man, free or slave, could race a horse in his name then, so Darley carried Dr. Warfield's colors and Dr. Warfield put up half the entrance fee for his first start on May 23, 1853, in Lexington. This was the annual mile-heat fixture for the best three-year-olds in the Bluegrass; since 1838 it had been known as the Phoenix Hotel Stakes. The proprietor of the Phoenix had wearied of being responsible for $100 worth of plate, however, and he had transferred the financial responsibility for a trophy to the track; for fourteen renewals the fixture was run as the Association Stakes.

Darley was entered against a dozen three-year-olds. He, favored Garrett Davis, and John Clay's Madonna broke away before the start and ran 2 1/4 miles before they could be pulled up. Garrett Davis appeared to be in great distress and was withdrawn on order of the judges, but Darley and Madonna were sent off with the field. The track was knee-deep in mud following a hard, two-day rain, but Darley flashed to the front, was never headed, and won the first heat in 1:55 1/2, distancing all but three others in the field. (In mile heats, the distance flag was located forty yards short of the finish line; horses which failed to beat the distance flag, by finishing within forty yards of the winner, were disqualified from subsequent heats to avoid anyone's "going for Sweeny," just galloping along the first heat so as to come out a fresh horse for later heats.) Darley won the second heat in the same manner, end-to-end, with John Harper's Wild Irishman second, John Campbell's Fanny Fern third, and Madonna distanced.

In attendance was Richard Ten Broeck, who owned most of the stock in the Metairie Course in New Orleans and who was on the lookout for horses to run in the Great State Post Stakes, an event he was promoting to draw representatives from each racing state, with a $5,000 entrance fee calculated to build the greatest prize ever raced for.

Several people had approached Dr. Warfield and offered to buy his colt. Ten Broeck tried and was turned down. Ten Broeck then formed a syndicate, including prominent Kentucky horsemen General Abe Buford, Junius R. Ward, and Captain Willa Viley. Ten Broeck offered $2,500 with another $2,500 to be paid if the colt won the Great State Post Stakes, coupled with the condition that the horse's name would be changed to Lexington and would represent Kentucky in the race. Dr. Warfield accepted. He did not tell Harry, his trainer, however, who went ahead and entered the horse as "Darley" for the Citizens' Stakes at two-mile heats scheduled four days after the 4 1/4-mile performance.

Inexplicably, "Darley" lost the first heat to John Harper's Boston filly, Midway, in 3:42 1/2. He came right back, however, to win the next two heats in 3:41 1/2 and 3:49, easily besting Midway and Garrett Davis while distancing four others. Although sold to Ten Broeck's syndicate, "Darley" ran in Dr. Warfield's name and carried his silks, and the breeder received nothing from the race; Harry had posted the entrance fee and received all the $1,300 purse while Captain Viley got the trophy, which today reposes on his grandson's mantel in Lexington.

Among those who had tried to buy Dr. Warfield's colt was Louis Smith, who wanted him to represent his state (Alabama) in the Great State Post Stakes. Earlier in the year, J. L. Pool of Mobile had a grand Glencoe filly, Sallie Waters, which had beaten Ten Broeck's Boston gelding, Arrow, in record time for three-mile heats. Ten Broeck did not count Arrow as fairly beaten, and Smith was somewhat chafed that Ten Broeck had outmaneuvered him on the purchase of Lexington. From this situation came a challenge from Smith, offering $5,000 against $3,500 that Sallie Waters could beat Lexington at three-mile heats.

Ten Broeck had shipped Lexington to John B. Pryor at Natchez for training. About the time Smith laid down his challenge, Lexington broke through his stall and into an adjacent feed room, gorging himself on corn. The next morning he was taken out for training and was in obvious distress. Returned to his stall, he collapsed and it was necessary to have him bled. His condition precluded any serious preparation for his match with Sallie Waters, and the filly, fresh from a victory in two-mile heats, was heavily favored when the two met on December 2 in New Orleans.

A writer for the *New Orleans Picayune* observed: "Upon stripping, the fine form of Sallie and the apparent excellence of her condition challenged the admiration of all. Lexington's appearance violates all laws of horsemen in the purchase of a horse—four white legs, glass or 'wall' eyes, and is a blazed young rip. His style of going, however, is the poetry of motion and the horse that outruns him in a sticky, heavy track, like that of yesterday, must be some sort of steam engine in disguise." Lexington won the first three-mile heat in 6:23 1/2 and distanced the filly in the second heat with a clocking of 6:24 1/2, "establishing the fact that despite his four white feet and white nose, he is one of the best racers that has shown here for many years."

Interest mounted in the coming Great State Post Stakes, for which at least nine states were expected to send representatives. New York, Virginia, North Carolina, South Carolina, and Tennessee failed to find representatives worth the $5,000 entrance fee, however, and on April 1, 1854, before some 20,000 spectators (including Millard Fillmore, only a year out of the White House), which was the largest crowd ever gathered at the Metairie Course in New Orleans, these four horses answered the call: Highlander, Alabama's four-year-old champion, the favorite; Lexington, unbeaten in three starts, co-second choice; Lecomte, unbeaten in five starts, co-second choice, representing Mississippi although foaled in Kentucky and bred and owned by Louisianian T. J. Wells; Arrow, another four-year-old, winner of five of his seven starts, representing Louisiana. Prior to 1858, southern racing rules determined horse's ages from May 1, rather than January 1 as now, so both Lexington and Lecomte carried the three-year-old weight of eighty-six pounds.

Lexington won easily. He took the track at the onset, followed by Arrow, Lecomte, and Highlander, and thus they went for the first mile. Lecomte challenged during the second mile, moving up beside Lexington, but then

27

Lexington pulled away. In the fourth mile, Arrow eased up and was distanced (eighty yards back for four-mile heats) as Lexington crossed the finish line three lengths in front of Lecomte.

For the second heat, Highlander set the pace for the first mile, then Lecomte took over and opened up an eight-length lead which he maintained during the second and third laps. On the fourth mile, Henry Meichon got into Lexington, closed the margin, caught Lecomte three furlongs from home, put him away, and drew off to win by four lengths.

"One could sadly misjudge the merits of this great contest by glancing at the time (8:08 3/4, 8:04) which we acknowledge would appear slow if the track had been in good condition," chronicled the *Picayune*. "Under the circumstances, the race was an excellent one; its varying chances, its uncertain termination up to the last moment, the severity of the contest, the amount of money at stake, and the immense number of persons in attendance will render it a brilliant event in the annals of this country."

Captain Viley, who had nominal charge of Lexington on behalf of the syndicate, decided Lexington would race no more that season, had his shoes removed, and turned him out in a paddock. Ten Broeck, interested in getting some of the Lecomte money which was showing for the Jockey Club Purse, scheduled for the following Saturday, was adamant that Lexington would run again. This impasse was resolved when Ten Broeck bought out the Kentuckians' interests for a reported $5,000. Lexington was reshod and on April 8 he was brought out for four-mile heats against General Wells's Lecomte and John Hunter's aged gelding from New York, Reube.

Lecomte was ridden by Abe, an accomplished jockey who had been purchased just before the Great State Post Stakes from Mississippi horseman A. L. Bingaman for $2,350. Lexington again was ridden by Henry Meichon, a less experienced Creole rider; Ten Broeck took him off after Lexington was defeated in the first heat (Ten Broeck later wrote to the *Spirit of the Times:* "The boy rode so badly he was exchanged for another, who was reclaimed by his owner after being dressed and the bell sounded for saddling for the second heat").

It seems doubtful whether Lexington's green rider had anything to do with Lexington's defeat in the first heat. Lecomte just outran him. Lecomte took command at the start and won by six lengths in world-record time of 7:26, beating by 6 1/2 seconds the record set by Fashion when she defeated Boston twelve years earlier. In the second heat, Lexington set the pace for the first two miles, leading by two lengths until Lecomte drew even in the third mile; Lecomte started the fourth mile with a daylight lead which suddenly lengthened when Meichon pulled up Lexington, thinking the race was over. Warned by the crowd of his mistake, Meichon started Lexington again, but he could get no closer than four lengths as Lecomte won in 7:38 3/4.

Lexington's defeat resulted in a succession of challenges and counterchallenges between Ten Broeck and General Wells, appearing in the form of nasty letters to the *Spirit of the Times.* Nothing much came of this. Ten Broeck shipped Lexington and Arrow north to run at the inaugural meeting of the National Course on Long Island. They were placed in the care of Captain William A. Stuart, quartered at the old Union Course on Long Island, but Stuart died of cholera and the pair then was shipped to Holmdel, New Jersey, in the care of Charles Lloyd. A few days before Lexington was to run in the Astor House Stakes in New York, his bridle broke while galloping on the training track and he veered off into a cornfield, so bruising his legs that it was necessary to take him out of training. He was returned south and placed again in the care of Pryor.

Since nothing came of the challenges to and from Lecomte's owner, Ten Broeck accepted a $20,000 challenge to run Lexington against Lecomte's record time of 7:26 for four miles. He brought in to ride Lexington the best jockey in the country, Gilbert Watson Patrick (who had ridden Boston in the 1840s and was to win the first Travers with Kentucky and the first Belmont with Ruthless in the 1860s under the name of Gilpatrick). Joe Blackburn tried to pace Lexington in the first mile, but was left behind; Arrow was sent up for the second and third miles, and Joe Blackburn came on again for the fourth. None of the pacemakers got near Lexington. He ran the four miles in 7:19 3/4, better than six seconds faster than Lecomte's time. He literally ran out of his shoes; one of them, twisted, now hangs in the National Museum of Racing at Saratoga.

Twelve days after Lexington beat Lecomte's time, the two rivals finally met again on April 14, 1855, at Metairie. As often happens in these long-awaited matches, one of the contestants came up amiss. Lecomte suffered an attack of colic. He was far from his best. He tried Lexington for three miles, but on the last lap Lexington spurted away and Lecomte barely failed to save his distance, beaten by almost eighty yards. Time for the race was 7:23 3/4, which again bettered Lecomte's former world mark. Lecomte was withdrawn from the second heat.

This was Lexington's final race. He had suffered loss of sight in his left eye as a result of getting into the feed room at Natchez as a three-year-old, and his right eye weakened so that he could see only vague outlines, necessitating his retirement to stud. With six wins in seven starts and earnings of $56,600, he was America's third-greatest money winner (Peytona had $62,400 and American Eclipse, $56,700). Ten Broeck sent him to Uncle John Harper's Nantura Stud near Midway, Kentucky, where Lexington stood his first two seasons.

R. A. Alexander, who had been touring Europe in quest of the best livestock in the world for his Woodburn Stud (adjacent to Nantura), chanced to meet Ten Broeck in England and from him purchased Lexington for $15,000. The price was considered high for a blind stallion whose first foals were sucklings, but Alexander vowed he would sell a colt by Lexington for more than his buying price. Seven years later, Alexander sold unbeaten Norfolk for $15,001. Lexington stood initially for $100, then $200, and in 1865 was raised to $500, highest stud fee in the United States.

Beginning in 1861 he led America's sire lists every year until he died in 1875 and then headed the list twice more posthumously, sixteen years in all. No stallion in the world so dominated his contemporaries: Italy's greatest sire, Havresac II, led ten times between 1924 and 1934 and England's greatest sire, St. Simon, led nine times between 1890 and 1901. Three stallions led for eight years: Glencoe in the United States between 1847 and 1858, Signorino in Italy between 1911 and 1923, and Bold Ruler in the United States between 1963 and 1973.

Lexington sired more good horses than any other stallion before or since. He was past his prime when Walter S. Vosburgh began designating champions after the Civil War, but by way of suggesting what Lexington's progeny did in his waning years: Kentucky was champion handicapper of 1865–1866, General Duke was champion three-year-old of 1868, Vauxhall was champion handicapper of 1869, Harry Bassett was champion of his age in 1870, 1871, and 1872, Tom Bowling was champion at two and three in 1872 and 1873, Acrobat was champion three-year-old in 1874, Sultana was the best three-year-old filly of 1876, and Duke of Magenta, from Lexington's next-to-last crop, was champion at two and three in 1877 and 1878.

The Travers Stakes at Saratoga started out as an important fixture and so remains today. Lexington's progeny owned the Travers: Kentucky won the first one in 1864, Maiden took the second running (she produced champion Parole and is the sixth dam of Nearco), Merrill won the third, The Banshee won it in 1868, Kingfisher in 1870, Harry Bassett in 1871, Tom Bowling in 1873, Sultana in

1876, and Duke of Magenta in 1878—nine of the first fifteen runnings of the Travers were won by sons and daughters of Lexington.

Lexington's ability as a stallion is incalculably better than his record shows. He happened to come along at a time when the Civil War destroyed racing, among other things. When Lexington was in his prime as a stallion, many of his progeny went into the cavalry, mares carrying his foals were stolen and lost, and racing opportunities were scant. Lexington's third through fifth crops were the result of matings with 218 mares and produced only twenty-four winners; as a usual thing these crops produce a stallion's best horses. Apparently most of Lexington's progeny from these crops went to war.

A hint of what Lexington was siring during the war years is revealed by Kentucky, Asteroid, and Norfolk, a troika of champion colts foaled in 1861. Not until Bull Lea sired Citation, Coaltown, and Bewitch in his 1945 crop did a stallion get three such horses in a single crop. Kentucky was the best horse in America for two or three years, winner of twenty-one of his twenty-two starts, beaten only by undefeated Norfolk in the inaugural Jersey Derby; Asteroid, competing in the Midwest, went undefeated in a dozen starts.

Of Lexington's 238 winners, eighty-four were top class, an arbitrary assessment perhaps comparable to stakes winners of today. Of these, eleven recognized champions were Idlewild, Kentucky, Asteroid, Norfolk, General Duke, Vauxhall, Harry Bassett, Tom Bowling, Acrobat, Sultana, and Duke of Magenta.

CITATION

A LAW OF GENETICS requires a return to the norm, that is, above-average individuals will tend to reproduce something less than they were, closer to the average, while inferior individuals will tend to reproduce something better, again closer to the norm. Thus, selective breeding of Thoroughbreds, mating an exceptional sire with a good broodmare to produce a better racehorse, is against the law. Man has been working on this for several centuries, however, and in flagrant violation of this law has indeed improved the breed of Thoroughbreds.

Today's racehorses are considerably taller and finer, faster and hardier, on the average, than were the general run of horses in 1540 when Henry VIII prohibited by law the breeding of mares smaller than fourteen hands; than in 1662 when Charles II rode Old Rowley to victory on the Round Course at Newmarket; than in 1780 when Diomed won the first English Derby; than in 1823 when American Eclipse beat Sir Henry in four-mile heats at Union Course on Long Island; than in 1923 when Kentucky Derby winner Zev defeated English Derby winner Papyrus at Belmont Park.

Thoroughbreds now stand taller, sixteen hands on the average; they run faster, ordinary horses now racing a mile in 1:35 compared to the American record in 1877 of 1:39 3/4 Ten Broeck set for the mile; and their bones and sinews are such as to withstand a stern training regime involving frequent fast works over hard dirt surfaces that their forebears probably could not have handled.

The suspicion here is that this gradual improvement over the centuries has not been the result so much of repeated selection of top individuals for mating, but rather the nonselection of inferior individuals—successive centuries of culling at the bottom. Colts that do not demonstrate exceptional speed and stamina on the race course do not command wide popularity as stock horses; inferior racing animals, generally, produce fewer progeny than do those which gain a reputation on the race course for superior abilities. A colt of undistinguished racing performance is lightly patronized by mare owners; often only the stallion's owner is optimistic enough to breed mares to him. If such a stallion does not sire outstanding runners in his initial crops, his stud career will be abandoned after siring but twenty or thirty foals. On the other hand, a distinguished runner when retired to stud may command some thirty or forty mares in his initial breeding season, and if some good performers result from these matings, such a stallion may sire as many as 500 foals during his lifetime. In short, more good racehorses are used for breeding than are bad horses, the majority of successive generations resulting from the mating of not-inferior racing stock. This, over the centuries, in a general way has raised the quality of the average Thoroughbred, the breed as a whole. The specifics within this general proposition, however, are more complex.

A man who sets out to breed a single great Thoroughbred faces some formidable challenges:

1) Time: A single man does not have a century or more at his disposal to work on the project; ten years without realizing some success saps financial resources and intellectual enthusiasm. Gestation period for a horse is eleven months, and mares on the average will have one barren year for every two foaling years. A Thoroughbred foal is

not eligible to race until two years of age, and he may not be able to demonstrate his racing potential until three or four years of age. In ten years, a mare may have only three foals that are old enough to race so as to demonstrate whether she is a good producer or a mare that should be culled. The culling of only one mare from a broodmare band will not in itself ensure the breeding of a single great Thoroughbred.

2) Probabilities: Heredity is an imprecise science, so abstruse as to defy man's attempts to develop a specific formula which can be applied to produce invariably a good horse; matings of the same parents in successive years do not produce identical results; none of John L. Sullivan's brothers could match his prowess in the ring, and none of Citation's full brothers or sisters could match his racing class. The only formula or guide breeders have is "to breed the best to the best, and hope for the best," an empirical method challenging such known percentages as: Only 59 percent of all Thoroughbred foals ever earn part of a purse; only 2.5 percent ever win a stakes race. The probability of breeding a good stakes winner is scant.

3) Money: Investment in Thoroughbred breeding stock is unlike investment in bank certificates of deposits which assure a set percentage of return in interest irrespective of the amount invested. A million-dollar investment in ten broodmares may be expected to realize a profitable return, whereas a $10,000 investment in ten broodmares cannot be expected to realize the same percentage of profit, and more often than not, will produce no profit. In 1973 two champion racehorses were sold as sire prospects, Secretariat at $6.08 million and Riva Ridge at $5.12 million; a top broodmare prospect, Typecast, was auctioned for $725,000; a yearling colt was auctioned as a racing prospect for $600,000.

In the history of the Turf, few men have met the challenges of time, probabilities, and money and enjoyed sustained success in breeding Thoroughbreds. None has succeeded to the extent of Warren Wright, master of Calumet Farm in Kentucky. Of America's most successful Thoroughbred breeders of this century, John E. Madden, August Belmont II, and Colonel E. R. Bradley never topped the list of winning racing owners; H. P. Whitney's stable of homebreds led the lists seven times, and his son, C. V. Whitney, ranked first five times. From 1941 through 1961, Calumet Farm was the leading racing stable twelve times, America's leading breeder fourteen times.

From 1898 through 1929, Madden bred 182 stakes winners at his Hamburg Place on the Winchester Pike near Lexington, including nine champions, only one of which raced in his colors. From 1891 through 1924, Belmont bred 129 stakes winners at his Nursery Stud on the Georgetown Pike near Lexington, including eight champions, only four of which raced in his colors. From 1905 through 1946, Bradley bred 128 stakes winners at his Idle Hour Stock Farm on the Old Frankfort Pike near Lexington, including fourteen champions, nine of which raced for him. From 1905 through 1930, H. P. Whitney bred 192 stakes winners at his farms in Red Bank, New Jersey, and on the Paris Pike near Lexington, including twenty champions. From 1930 through 1974, C. V. Whitney bred 156 stakes winners at his farm on the Paris Pike near Lexington, including three champions.

From 1931 until his death in 1950, Warren Wright bred seventy-five stakes winners including eleven champions at his Calumet Farm on the Versailles Pike near Lexington; since his death, the breeding stock at Calumet Farm has been managed by his widow, now Mrs. Gene Markey, and has produced another sixty-four stakes winners and three more champions for a Calumet total of 139 stakes winners, including fourteen champions.

Warren Wright, although starting from scratch in Thoroughbred breeding and racing in 1931, had the jump on other men starting from scratch. For one thing, he had inherited some $70 million including a 900-acre Standardbred breeding nursery his father had named after the baking powder company he had founded. For another, he decided to devote his full time and considerable business acumen—he was the primary person responsible for the growth of the family business to the point where he could sell it to General Foods in 1928 for $28 million—to converting Calumet Farm from a prominent harness racing and breeding operation into a highly successful Thoroughbred nursery. Seldom does a man with almost unlimited financial resources and a habit of business success direct his undivided attention toward breeding and racing top Thoroughbreds; Warren Wright demonstrated what could be done with these tools.

A small, dapper, humorless man, Wright was brought into Thoroughbred racing by John D. Hertz as part owner of Arlington Park in Chicago. Hertz, self-made millionaire founder of the Yellow Cab Company, had entered racing auspiciously as the owner-breeder of the champion two-year-olds of 1927, the colt Reigh Count, which was to win the Kentucky Derby the next year, and the filly Anita Peabody. Hertz recommended to Wright his first broodmare purchase, Nellie Morse, one of the few fillies to win the important Preakness Stakes; purchased from cartoonist Bud Fisher ("Mutt and Jeff"), Nellie Morse was carrying a foal by American Flag at the time.

The resultant foal, a filly born in 1932 at Calumet Farm and named Nellie Flag, was the first Thoroughbred ever bred by Wright. At two, Nellie Flag became Wright's first stakes winner and first champion; later as a broodmare, Nellie Flag produced a champion mare which in turn produced top runners. This is an improbable sequence which nonetheless set a pattern at Calumet Farm, where the improbability of such success became probable.

Warren Wright picked out a great stallion as a yearling. The odds against this happenstance are incalculable. In North America 546,878 Thoroughbreds have been registered as foaled from 1900 through 1971. Of these, 270,174 were colts, and of these only twenty emerged as highly successful stallions, successful to the extent of siring as

37

many as forty stakes winners during their stud careers. Of these twenty stallions, only four or five may be termed "great" stallions. So in frequency, during three-quarters of a century, four or five great stallions emerged from 270,174 male foals; this is an expectancy of one great stallion for every 54,035 colts.

Thus the odds against selecting a great stallion as a yearling are formidable, but at the 1936 Saratoga yearling sale, Wright did happen to select and purchase for $14,000 a colt by Bull Dog–Rose Leaves, by Ballot, consigned by Coldstream Stud of Lexington. Through the years, although Wright selected other yearling colts with the same care and deliberation, and with the same high expectation of subsequent racing and breeding success, the colts came to naught. The $14,000 Bull Dog colt, however, proved to be a nice racehorse and a great sire. Wright named him Bull Lea, and he became the foundation for Calumet's success.

At two, Bull Lea won only two minor races in nine starts, but finished second to the two best colts of the season in the Hopeful and Champagne stakes and was rated fifth on the year-end handicap ranking of the crop. At three, he set a track record in defeating champion Menow in the Blue Grass Stakes, and although he won three other stakes later in the year, was never as good as he was in the spring; at season's end, he again was rated fifth among a relatively undistinguished crop of colts. At four, he ran only twice, winning the prestigious Widener Handicap in Florida, but suffered from ankle trouble and was retired with ten wins in twenty-seven starts and earnings of $94,825, a respectable but not outstanding racing record, one that gave little indication of his extraordinary success as a stallion. He was to become America's leading sire five times, siring an exceptional number of stakes winners, fifty-eight, nine of which were champions—Durazna, Twilight Tear, Armed, Citation, Bewitch, Coaltown, Two Lea, Next Move, and Real Delight—plus Kentucky Derby winners Hill Gail and Iron

Liege, Preakness winner Faultless, and top horses such as Mark-Ye-Well, Level Lea, Gen. Duke, Alerted, Miz Clementine, and Bubbley.

Bull Lea was second favorite for the 1938 Kentucky Derby, and finished a disappointing eighth. The winner, Lawrin, was saddled by trainer Ben A. Jones and ridden by Eddie Arcaro. Wright noticed that. Success in the horse business, like success in almost any business, depends upon people. Wright had tried a succession of capable trainers—Willie Knapp, Danny Stewart, Bert Williams, and Frank Kearns—none of whom had attained the degree of success with the Calumet racing stable Wright was seeking. The racing and breeding operation was in the black, but not much ink was being used. Wright approached Ben Jones with an offer to train the Calumet horses.

"Mr. Wright," Jones said, "I'm afraid your horses aren't good enough." Wright turned devil red, lacking only blue hoops on his sleeves to match his stable silks.

"Well, by George, if I'm not raising them good enough, I'll buy them for you," Wright declared.

Jones thought to himself, "Now here's a man who wants to go some place," and he shook hands on the deal that was to be significant for both men. This was 1939, and Jones already had been to more than a few places, none of them very important in a racing way, but enough to provide Jones with a reputation bordering on legend as to his knowledge of horses, training, medication, placement, and ability to survive in the rough-and-tumble world that was known as bush racing.

Born on the last day of 1882 on his father's 2,500-acre cattle farm near Parnell, Missouri, Jones grew up liking both horses and Holstein cows. "Couldn't decide which I liked better," Jones recalled, "but when I got big enough to help with the milking, I made up my mind."

Jones was sent to the State Agriculture College of Colorado to gain formal training to help his father with an extensive cattle operation or in the family bank at Parnell,

39

but it did not take. Jones's interest in the farm was restricted to the half-mile training track in the cornfield there, and his idea of a bright future was winning the $1,000 purse put up for the next summer's Sioux City Derby. He started at local fairs, matching running horses at 200 or 400 yards. "I used to think a half-mile was a long race," Jones said in recalling his early racing days. He won his first race at a 5/8-mile track in Fort Worth and won at Tulsa, Lewiston, and at nearly all the two-day meetings in the West where he scrambled for $100 purses. In 1909 when Colonel Matt Winn opened a race meeting in Juarez, Mexico, young Ben Jones was there with several horses.

"Had the best time in my whole life at Juarez. Times were tough then, and when Colonel Winn said there was going to be $400 minimum purses, I thought the world was coming to an end. There just wasn't any money around then . . . at least I didn't have any. We lived in the barns, and boarded at Dick Lee's kitchen—$3.50 a week for 21 meals—an old adobe building behind the track with a clay floor and three tables with benches on both sides. I won a bet and went over to Lee's, gave him $20 and told him to take care of my help; Lee says, 'Come over here B. A. and let me kiss you. This is the first cash I've seen in a month!'

"Raced there every winter. In 1916, Pancho Villa took over the town and I heard he was coming out to the track to pick up some black horses. I had a black horse I depended on, named Lemon Joe, could run like the devil. If they took him, they took my whole stable. Had a 10-pound sack of mud hanging outside his door, used to pack his feet with to keep moisture in there because he had shelly feet, and I just took that whole sack, jammed his front right in it and tied the string around his ankle. Soldiers came down the shedrow, opened the door on Lemon Joe, saw him limping around with that 10 pounds of mud and just shook their heads. Took a little black mare in the next stall, belonged to Mrs. Armstrong who ran a

40

boarding house there, but took one of my bridles and saddles."

Jones usually raced about a dozen horses in this period, in Juarez, Cuba, New Orleans in the winter, Canada in the summer, mostly horses he had bred in Missouri, by stallions now forgotten such as His Lordship, Blues, Harrigan, and Waldo. His best stallion, Seth, was purchased for $800 from Carroll Shilling's brother. Virtually all Seth's progeny raced for Jones; Seth ranked among America's twenty leading sires from 1925 through 1928 and was tied as leading sire of two-year-olds in 1929. Jones gained renown as a miracle man with two-year-olds, opening each season in Cuba, or Florida, or New Orleans by winning the first races of the year with two-year-olds by Seth. "We had to win in a hurry then; needed the money, living day to day." As a breeder, Jones never ranked lower than ninth in the nation in number of races won from 1922 through 1931. From 1917 through 1945 horses bred by Jones won 3,049 races.

None of these winners bred and raced by Jones commanded much national attention. In 1932, "I was doing bad, my stable was not winning many races, and the depression was hurting everybody. Then one day Herbert Woolf, who owned the department store in Kansas City and had a lot of money, asked me to take over his stable. Seemed at the time a good idea, to have him pay all the bills rather than my hustling all the time, so I sold all my horses and went to work for the Woolford Stable."

With Herbert Woolf, Jones moved to the major racing circuits. He began with an established champion mare, Lady Broadcast, and at Hialeah, New York, Chicago, and California, Jones developed champion fillies Inscoelda and Unerring, plus such top runners as Joe Schenck, Technician, and Lawrin. Thus when Warren Wright approached Jones to train the Calumet horses, he was talking to a man with more than thirty-years' experience breeding, owning, and training horses for himself and others, ordinary horses and good horses, at minor tracks

41

and major tracks, in bad times and good times; in short, a man for all racing seasons.

In the fall of 1939 Jones arrived in Kentucky to look over the first Calumet yearlings he was to train. Among these was a little chestnut colt with a tail that was to grow long and storied; this was Whirlaway, in the first American crop of foals sired by Blenheim II, in which Wright had purchased a quarter interest when the celebrated English Derby winner was imported to stand at Claiborne Farm in Kentucky. Whirlaway was out of Dustwhirl, a mare Wright had purchased after she had produced a good stakes winner in Reaping Reward. Jones developed Whirlaway into the champion two-year-old of 1940 when his earnings of $77,275 made up more than half of the stable's earnings that raised Calumet up to third place on the owners' list for the year. In 1941 Jones saddled Whirlaway for victories in the Kentucky Derby, Preakness, and Belmont Stakes, the first of two Triple Crowns for Calumet. The Kentucky Derby, America's most famous horse race, was to be won by a three-year-old bred and owned by Calumet a record eight times: by Whirlaway in 1941, by Pensive in 1944, by Citation in 1948, by Ponder in 1949, by Hill Gail in 1952, by Iron Liege in 1957, by Tim Tam in 1958, and by Forward Pass upon a disqualification in 1968. The Preakness was to be won by a Calumet three-year-old a record seven times: by Whirlaway in 1941, by Pensive in 1944, by Faultless in 1947, by Citation in 1948, by Fabius in 1956, by Tim Tam in 1958, and by Forward Pass in 1968. The Belmont was won by Calumet's two Triple Crown winners, Whirlaway in 1941 and Citation in 1948.

With Whirlaway, the Calumet dynasty began. From 1940 through 1961 Calumet topped the owners' list a dozen times, ranked second four times, and third twice. In 1957, when no other racing stable in the world ever had earned purses amounting to as much as a million dollars during a single year, Calumet stable earnings passed that earnings mark for the sixth time. Earning a

Citation, after winning the Flamingo Stakes as a three-year-old, was greeted in the winner's circle by trainers Ben A. Jones and son Jimmy.

Warren Wright, master of Calumet Farm

million dollars in a year is not uncommon in recent times, but it might be noted that in 1948, when Calumet earned $1,269,710, the second-leading stable earned only $490,832; and in 1952, when Calumet earned $1,283,197, the second-leading stable earned less than half that sum, $600,505.

In short, Calumet Farm had the horses, with as many as ten or eleven different stakes winners racing at the same time from a barn of horses numbering from thirty-four to fifty; one or more Calumet runners were voted champion in twelve of thirteen consecutive years including Whirlaway, the first horse to earn $500,000; Armed, the first gelding to earn $800,000; Bewitch, the first filly to earn as much as $460,000; and Citation, the first horse to earn more than $1 million.

Of all the good horses Warren Wright bred and owned, of all the good horses trained by Ben Jones and his son Jimmy, of all the good horses ridden by Eddie Arcaro, Citation was the best.

Citation was foaled April 11, 1945, at Calumet Farm. He was by five-time leading sire, Bull Lea, out of a mare imported from England, Hydroplane II, by the celebrated Hyperion, six-time leading sire. It is customary to color this breeding purple, but it should be noted that the same breeding, Bull Lea and Hydroplane II, produced four foals: one great racehorse in Citation, and three others whose want of inherited running ability defies recollection of their names.

Citation was broken along with twenty-nine other yearlings in the fall of 1946 on the six-furlong training track at Calumet Farm, then shipped to Hialeah in the winter where the stable was to begin a record year: In 1947 Calumet's six-year-old gelding, Armed, was voted champion handicapper and Horse of the Year; Bewitch was voted champion two-year-old filly; Citation was voted champion two-year-old colt; Faultless won the classic Preakness; Fervent, Twosy, Free America, Whirl Some, Pep Well, and Pot o' Luck each won stakes. Thirty-six horses in the Calumet stable won 100 races and earned $1,402,436, a record sum unsurpassed for twenty-three years—and then by reason of inflationary purses rather than quality of runners.

In such a stable, there was little need to do much early with a nice two-year-old colt, and Citation was not raced that winter in Florida, but sent with a division of the stable in the care of Jimmy Jones to Maryland in the spring when Ben Jones took the main division to Kentucky. Father and son worked closely in handling the Calumet horses, Ben under the formal title of general manager while Jimmy was listed as trainer.

The trade press with simple directness lists the trainer of a horse as the individual who happens to saddle it for a particular race. At times, Citation was saddled by each of the Joneses. With Jimmy in Maryland, Citation won his first start on April 22 at the old Havre de Grace track, then won two other minor races in Maryland during May and was put away for two months. When the stable divisions were rejoined in July in Chicago, Ben Jones again turned his attention to Citation. In preparation for his first stakes venture, Citation was sent out on July 24 in an allowance affair and came back quickly, five furlongs in fifty-eight seconds, setting a new track record at Arlington Park. A week later, he won his first stakes, the $20,000-added Elementary Stakes, defeating good colts in Salmagundi, Billings, Pinebloom, and Papa Redbird.

Then came the Washington Park Futurity. Calumet had such strength in the two-year-old division at the time that the Joneses sent out three horses, and finished 1-2-3 in the field of ten.

"We kind of figured our horses could take the first three places, so we told the riders before the race we'd split the jockey fees three ways between them; whoever was in front was to be allowed to win the thing without any of the three boys to go whipping a horse to death just to get a bigger riding fee," Jimmy Jones later recalled.

"Well, Bewitch got out there—she could go five furlongs in 58 seconds almost any time she wanted—and so Citation just sort of galloped along. Bewitch kind of slowed, though, in the stretch and Citation picked up five lengths on her very easily to finish second by a length, with Free America only a head back in third place. When the riders came back to unsaddle after the race, Doug Dodson, who was on Bewitch, said he could have gone on and pulled away any time he wanted, but Steve Brooks said, 'Naw, Citation was just loafing; we could have gone right by your filly.' About that time Jackie Westrope got back with Free America and said, 'You guys are just kidding yourselves. I coulda taken both of you without even going to the whip!' "

This was to be Citation's only loss at two, and that was not so much a defeat as a deference to a stablemate. Shipped to New York, Citation won the Futurity Trial over favored My Request and five days later was coupled with Bewitch in a field of fourteen drawn for the year's most important race for two-year-olds, the Futurity. With but a furlong left in the race, six horses were no more than a length apart when Citation made his move, drawing off to win by three lengths.

A month later Citation was asked to race beyond a mile, a question always posed to good two-year-olds when thoughts turn toward next season's classic races. In the Pimlico Futurity, Citation handled 1 1/16 miles of deep mud, plus such nice colts as Better Self, Ace Admiral, and Royal Blood, with no trouble at all, concluding the season with eight wins in nine starts, and promise.

While he had been a solid two-year-old champion, there was no reason to expect anything more from Citation at three than was expected, say, from earlier champions Pavot or Bimelech, both of which were unbeaten at two. Citation's first two starts as a three-year-old, however, suggested a greatness the Turf had not seen since Man o' War. At Hialeah on February 2, he was brought out for a six-furlong race against really good older horses (which is comparable to asking a star junior high school basketball player to scrimmage against college players).

"Tell you how that came about," Jimmy Jones recalled later. "I had let up on Citation after his race in the mud at Pimlico in November, had done very little with him for six weeks. Then at Hialeah, Eddie Moore showed with a real fast colt named Relic that had won the Hopeful Stakes at two, and won the Hibiscus Stakes in January in only two-fifths of a second off the track record. Mr. Wright was a close friend of Mr. Moore's, but they had this rivalry, you know, and Mr. Wright tells me he wants to run against Mr. Moore's colt—but he doesn't want to get Citation beat!

"Well, I was a young man then, didn't know too much, and I kinda took that as an order. I got to thinking: Relic already has a race in him and has the edge on Citation in that respect. So, I got to looking around for a spot, a little sprint race that didn't amount to anything, and finally found one. But it was open to older horses and we ran into some really good ones: Kitchen Police was five and we had to give him actual weight; Say Blue was four and she already had won $100,000; Tavistock was four and had won $100,000 in New York; and Rampart was a grand old mare that won the Black Helen and Gulfstream Park Handicap that year.

"Citation, though, could meet a challenge better than any other horse I ever knew. He let Kitchen Police take the lead for the first half, then came around him and won by a length pretty easily. Relic came back two days later, though, and won the Bahamas Stakes in time less than a second off the track record. Knowing how Mr. Wright wanted to beat that colt, I figured I had better find another little race for Citation before hooking Relic. Well, there just wasn't another race restricted to three-year-olds real soon, so I had to run him in the Seminole Handicap against some more tough older sprinters, like Delegate, and Buzfuz, and Round View. I ran Faultless and Armed, just in case it was too tough a spot for a three-year-old, but Citation didn't need them; he took old Delegate and ran

47

him into the ground. We figured we really were ready for Relic then—but don't you know, Relic broke down and we never did run against him."

Sunny Jim Fitzsimmons, who in his seventy years around the race track had seen Sysonby and Colin and had saddled a legion of good horses including two Triple Crown winners, was asked what he thought of Citation in February of 1948: "Up to this point, Citation has done more than any horse I ever saw." Then he paused. "And I saw Man o' War."

Citation thereupon was turned loose against horses of his own age, winning the Everglades Handicap and then the Flamingo Stakes by six lengths. His regular rider, Al Snider, who had ridden Citation to nine victories, went fishing after the Flamingo and never returned; his small craft was swept out to sea in a storm. Eddie Arcaro, winner of three Kentucky Derbys, two for Ben Jones, was called to ride Citation. He promptly lost with him.

"I could have caught Saggy that day," Arcaro said later, "but that was the first time I ever rode him, and I knew if I burned him out getting an $8,300 purse with all those $100,000 races ahead of him, Ben Jones never would let me ride him again." That was in the Chesapeake Trial. The next week in the Chesapeake Stakes, Arcaro brought Citation down with no trouble at all, beating Saggy by more than fifteen lengths. They headed for Kentucky where Ben Jones had a division of the Calumet stable which included a three-year-old said to be the fastest horse ever to race in America. This was Coaltown.

Coaltown had not raced as a two-year-old. He contracted a cold which developed into an abscess in his throat; this broke while he was exercising one morning in Chicago. He choked and fell on the track. "I rode over and looked at him," Ben Jones recalled. "He was lying there with blood and puss running out of his nostrils, and you wouldn't have given a hundred dollars for him. I wouldn't have bet we'd get him back to the barn." No one offered $100 and he did get back to the barn. A solution was used to keep his throat clear and Coaltown was put back in training, but Jones heard a rumbling noise in Coaltown's head and sent him back to Calumet Farm for the rest of the year.

As a three-year-old, Coaltown made his first start at Hialeah and there was a suspicion that he had left the starting gate before it opened for the rest of the horses, inasmuch as Coaltown had sprinted to an eight-length lead before a race really could develop. He won his next start by twelve lengths. Tried then against older stakes horses in the historic Phoenix Handicap at Lexington, Coaltown demonstrated that he did not need to take the track at once, coming between older rivals to win by 2 1/2 lengths. Tried next for distance, Coaltown opened up a quick six-length lead on serious Kentucky Derby candidates in the 1 1/8-mile Blue Grass Stakes and coasted home, breaking a ten-year Keeneland track record for the distance.

About this time it was decided by old-time horsemen, who conducted nightly seminars on racing matters in a corner of the Lafayette Hotel in Lexington, that no horse alive could beat Coaltown—except maybe his stablemate. After Citation won the mile Derby Trial four days before the Kentucky Derby, the only question that remained was which Calumet colt would win the big one. Place and show betting windows at Churchill Downs were closed for the race, since only four other horses were entered, perhaps with the hope that the Calumet pair would bump ten yards from the finish and fall down.

Jimmy Jones, in Maryland with Citation, had heard the talk of the brilliant colt his father was developing in Kentucky, and when Coaltown sprinted out to a six-length lead around the first turn in the Kentucky Derby, he thought, "Oh, oh, Dad's put one over on me again, this colt looks better than what he told me." Straightening out for the backstretch run, however, Arcaro clucked to Citation, closed the margin, and was at Coaltown's throatlatch after a mile. The pair wheeled into the homestretch on

49

even terms, and then Citation just galloped on, drawing off to win by 3 1/2 lengths from his stablemate.

During this era, the New York Yankees won the American League pennant routinely, prompting the plea, "Break up the Yankees!" In the spring of 1948 this cry was directed at Calumet. This was a mistake. After finishing 1–2 in the Kentucky Derby, Jimmy Jones took Citation to Baltimore and Ben Jones took Coaltown and a few other Calumet horses to New York. On May 15 Citation won the Preakness by 5 1/2 lengths in Baltimore, while Ben Jones saddled Faultless and Fervent to finish 1–2 in the rich Gallant Fox Handicap in New York. It became apparent that if the Calumet stable were broken up much further, there would be no important stakes purses left to anyone else.

Since there was little else for the Calumet colt to do during the month between the Preakness and Belmont Stakes that year, Citation stopped off at Garden State Park and casually won the $50,000-added Jersey Stakes by eleven lengths, slashing 1 3/5 seconds off the track record for 1 1/4 miles, and then went on to New York. Until a horse actually demonstrates his class at 1 1/2 miles, doubt always exists as to his range, and seven presumptuous challengers opposed Citation for the Belmont Stakes. He won by an unequivocal eight lengths, the second Triple Crown for Warren Wright, for the Joneses, and for Arcaro.

To the relief of all horsemen in town, Calumet then shipped out of New York and put the heat on Chicago. Giving weight to good older horses again, Citation equaled the track record in winning the Stars and Stripes Handicap, but he wrenched a muscle and did not race again for six weeks. After galloping in a prep race, he took the American Derby, finishing eight lengths in front of his stablemate Free America. Shipped back to New York, he was coupled with Coaltown again, which had just won the Jerome Handicap, in the Sysonby Mile. Sprinter Spy Song winged off on the lead, and Citation was six lengths back; Arcaro said he just clucked to his horse, but some-thing else must have happened, for within a furlong, Citation picked up six lengths on the best speed horses in training and drew off to win by three lengths from cham-pion filly First Flight, with Coaltown third.

Citation then was tried at two miles against a field of stayers the quality of which Man o' War probably never met: Phalanx, champion three-year-old of the previous season; Miss Grillo, an Argentine mare that excelled at long distances; and Conniver, champion handicap mare that year. Citation opened up a five-length lead, easily withstood some abortive challenges from sprinters, then turned back Conniver's bid, and when Phalanx came with his late charge, moved away with authority to win by seven lengths. Two weeks later in the 1 5/8-mile Empire City Gold Cup, Citation summarily disposed of Phalanx and Miss Grillo again, with Irish St. Leger winner Nathoo and Belgian champion Bayeux far back up the track.

In those days the Pimlico Special was run in No-vember, invitations being extended to the best horses in training to decide the year's championship on the race track, where it should be, rather than in polls. When an invitation was accepted for Citation, no one else showed up, and he galloped over the course all by himself.

This should have concluded his season, but a friend of Wright asked him, as a favor, to run Citation at Tanforan in San Francisco; thus a month later record crowds watched the champion win a six-furlong overnight purse and then take the Tanforan Handicap, setting a new track record for 1 1/4 miles.

That was the last of the towering greatness of Citation. He had done it all as a three-year-old: He had given weight to good older horses, at all distances, in all types of going; he had shown he could take the track and lead all the way or come from far behind; he had set or equaled four track records and, in winning nineteen of twenty starts from February 2 through December 11, had earned a season-record $709,470. Veteran Max Hirsch, who had trained or seen all the good racehorses of a half-century, stated flatly: "There's never been a horse like Citation."

Citation did not race as a four-year-old. He developed an osselet, a bony growth around an ankle, and although brought back at five and six, it was not back to what he had been. During Citation's absence, Coaltown won all the races Citation would have been pointed for, proving to be better than an average replacement. Coaltown won twelve of his first thirteen races as a four-year-old, broke four track records and set or equaled three world records, and was voted champion handicap horse of the year. It further amplifies Calumet's position in racing—to lose a Citation and still have four divisional champions in Coaltown, Wistful, Two Lea, Bewitch, and seven other stakes winners, and to top the owners' list again in 1949 with earnings of $1,128,942.

Although just a shell of what he had been, Citation was still a very good horse at five, and Wright thought a few of California's rich purses would put Citation ahead of Stymie as the world's greatest money winner. He won his first start as a five-year-old, a minor event at six furlongs, missed by a neck giving Miche sixteen pounds, then finished second to his younger stablemate Ponder in the San Antonio Handicap, finishing a half-length in front of an imported horse, Noor.

For the 1 1/4-mile Santa Anita Handicap, Noor carried 110 pounds, Citation 132, and Noor beat him by 1 1/4 lengths, setting a new track record. For the 1 3/4-mile San Juan Capistrano Handicap a week later, Noor carried 117 pounds, Citation 130, and Noor got up to beat him by a nose, reducing the track record by 5 4/5 seconds to 2:52 4/5, an American record. Shipped to San Francisco, Citation was put into a six-furlong overnight affair named the Surprise Purse, and a horse called Roman In ran a world-record 1:08 3/5 at him, Citation finishing second.

Two weeks later, Citation was brought out for the $20,000-added Golden Gate Mile Handicap against the grand sprinter Bolero. Bolero reeled off world-record fractions of :22 1/5 for the quarter, :44 1/5 for the half, and 1:07 3/5 for three-quarters of a mile; Bolero then began to get a little rubbery and veered out on the last turn, carrying Citation with him. Steve Brooks finally got Citation around Bolero, however, and brought Citation down to the wire in 1:33 3/5, breaking the world record for the mile that Coaltown had set a year earlier and at the same time surpassing Stymie's world earnings mark, the $14,550 winner's share of the purse upping Citation's career earnings to $924,631.

"We probably should not have kept going with him," Jimmy Jones recalled later. "We never really gave him enough time—you know you have to give a cripple more time to come back. I always seemed to be about two weeks behind in my training of him then, but although he was being beaten back to second, he never was beaten bad. Noor just kept improving."

For the 1 1/8-mile Forty-Niners Handicap, Noor carried 123 pounds, Citation 128, and Noor took him by a neck margin, setting another world record. The following week in the 1 1/4-mile Golden Gate Handicap, Noor gave Citation weight for the first time, one pound, and beat him by three lengths, setting another world record. Citation raced no more that year, in nine starts having won two and finished second seven times, his last six races being in record times.

Warren Wright died on December 28, 1950. He had hoped that Citation would be the first horse to earn a million dollars, and at the time Citation was $61,370 shy of the mark. Mrs. Wright asked the Joneses if they thought Citation could do it as a six-year-old; they thought he could.

At six, Citation lost his first four races to ordinary horses, but on June 14 at Hollywood Park, he won the mile Argonaut Handicap and then took the 1 1/8-mile American Handicap to raise his earnings to $985,760. Ten days later came the 1 1/4-mile Hollywood Gold Cup;

Citation took command early and came down four lengths in front of his champion stablemate Bewitch. It was his thirty-second victory in his forty-fifth race, raising his earnings to a record $1,085,760.

"I wanted to run him again," Jimmy Jones said. "He was just getting good again, and there was a $50,000 race there, just for the taking, but Mrs. Wright called me and said to send him home, because that was the way Mr. Wright would have wanted it."

At stud, Citation proved less successful than was expected. Upon his death in 1970 he had sired a champion filly in Silver Spoon, a Preakness winner in Fabius, and some nice stakes winners in Get Around, Watch Your Step, Manteau, Evening Time, Recite, Keenation, Carmel, Beyond, In Dispatches, and Sky Clipper—but nothing, really, that approached the greatness that was Citation.

DOMINO

THOROUGHBRED racing and breeding today is a distinct and important industry of significant social and economic impact in the United States. During 1973 more than $339 million in state tax revenue was generated by pari-mutuel wagering on 62,264 Thoroughbred races attended by more than 51 million persons. Thoroughbred racing now is conducted under state supervision in twenty-nine states where government agencies known as racing commissions grant licenses to race tracks and to participants in racing, allocate days as to when and where racing may be conducted, and promulgate racing rules with which all licensees must comply to participate.

All the 54,812 horses participating in these races must have been registered as Thoroughbreds by The Jockey Club in New York, their owners having in their possession a registration certificate verifying a pedigree "With eight crosses of pure blood, tracing back for at least a century, and to show such performances of its recent family on the turf as to justify the belief in the purity of its blood." Purses, derived from a small percentage of the pari-mutuel wagering pools (and in the instance of stakes races, nomination and entry fees of horse owners), amounted in 1973 to more than $233 million. The opportunity to earn such purse money—Kelso, from 1959 through 1966, won thirty-nine races and earned $1,977,896—has raised the

monetary value of Thoroughbreds solely for racing pur-
poses far above their value in former days when they
were bred and raced to improve the speed and stamina of
draft animals, road horses, and cavalry mounts. In 1973 all
yearlings, of varying promise auctioned in North America
averaged $12,255, and one was auctioned for $600,000; a
good broodmare prospect was auctioned for $725,000; a
great racehorse was syndicated as a sire prospect for
$6.08 million. A large number of people now devote their
entire lives to the business of breeding, raising, and
racing Thoroughbreds.

This was not the case a century ago. Horse racing was a
divertissement, a small amusement to a few men on a
local basis, comparable today to barrel racing at county
fairs. It generated no tax revenue; there was no pari-mutuel wagering, just man-to-man side wagers between
confident horse owners. There was no government regu-
lation; what rules there were, were locally imposed by
individual clubs that conducted the short race meetings.
Whereas now, some 28,000 Thoroughbreds are foaled
and registered each year, only 3,950 horses were foaled
from 1803 through 1892 that are listed in the *American
Stud Book* as Thoroughbreds—and these were so desig-
nated retroactively.

There was no official registry for American Thoroughbreds until The Jockey Club was formed in 1894 and
purchased the rights to Colonel Sanders D. Bruce's six-
volume set of what he called the *American Stud Book.*
Colonel Bruce collected what pedigrees he could of the
racehorses he knew about and published these in his first
two volumes in 1873. The integrity of these pedigrees is
in direct proportion to the integrity of the horse owners
who supplied them.

Purses were small, $400 as a common amount. Whereas
today top horses are flown from New York to California, or
from Florida to Chicago, for a single race, and entire
stables are vanned from New Orleans to Canada and back

again during the course of a year, racing prior to the Civil War was largely a local affair; even the best racers seldom ventured out of the state. A big price for a racehorse was $1,000; Lexington, the best horse in his day, was sold for $5,000—in two installments; he was resold as a stallion for a record $15,000 in 1857.

In short, racing was a sport, not a government-regulated business, a century ago. No one devoted their entire lives and business endeavor to breeding and racing horses; it was a sideline, in which a relatively few wealthy land-owners, lawyers, and doctors indulged themselves a few weeks out of the year. Kentucky racing men had much the same interest in chicken fighting and card playing; horse racing just was more visible, a gambling proposition played outdoors on a large track, sometimes commanding notice in local newspapers. Further, it had redeeming social qualities which chicken fighting and card playing lacked, in that those horses which proved to be the fastest and strongest on the race course could be used as stock animals to improve the breed of all horses.

Major Barak G. Thomas, retiring at the age of fifty after serving eight years as master commissioner and sheriff of Fayette County, was one of the first Lexingtonians to devote all his attention and resources to the breeding and racing of Thoroughbreds. He was educated as an at-torney, attending Indiana University and Transylvania University, obtaining his law degree from Transylvania in 1849. His older brother, Charles B. Thomas, was a prominent member of the Lexington bar; after serving as city judge, he was elected circuit judge for Fayette and surrounding counties in 1860, remaining on the bench until his death in 1873, except for a tour of duty as judge advocate with the Army of Virginia. Barak Thomas prac-ticed law but briefly, accepting a job as a civil engineer for the building of the Lexington & Frankfort Railroad, the first railroad west of the Alleghenies, and then serving as general freight and passenger agent in Lexington for twelve years. In 1861, when Lexington was occupied by Union troops, Thomas settled a disturbance outside the station by shooting and wounding a Union soldier. He made two quick decisions at that point: to join the Confederate Army, and to leave town. He did so, leaving that night and enlisting as a private in General Kirby-Smith's command. He immediately was assigned to General Abe Buford, a longtime friend and racing man from Woodford County, under whom Thomas rose in rank and served as commissary until 1863; at that time he was transferred as chief of commissary to General Joe Wheeler's Cavalry Corps, from which he was discharged as a major on May 3, 1865.

Major Thomas returned to Lexington and found most of his assets had been sold for debt during his absence. His most significant possession, he discovered, was a yearling filly. Major Thomas nearly always had one or two horses, acquiring his first at the age of nineteen as a reward for tracking down and recovering a mare and foal stolen by Indians from Dr. George Sanders. Young Thomas visited Indian camps in Scott and Jessamine counties and finally found the mare, Occidenta, by Bertrand, and her colt by Alex Churchill, at Camp Nelson. Dr. Sanders gave Thomas the colt which he named Wandering Willie and subsequently raced with some success. He also had raced, with his brother as partner, a mare by imported Ambassador named Hegira that in 1850 at New Orleans had established the American record for two miles, 3:34 1/2; this mare, bred to mighty Lexington, had produced the yearling filly to which the Thomas brothers returned after the war. Named Hira, the filly won the Proprietor's Stakes at the old Woodlawn Course in Louisville, racing in Judge Thomas's name. The victory, in her only start as a three-year-old, was worth $1,750, a considerable sum under the circumstances, and provided some indication as to her prospective value as a broodmare.

Major Thomas owned some cotton land in Arkansas,

which he traded for a six-year-old mare named Dixie, by imported Sovereign; Dixie did not have an opportunity to race during the war, but she proved to be a marvelous broodmare. Bred to Vandal, in 1866 she produced a colt Major Thomas named Herzog, but which, after frostbite marred the appearance of his ears, was known generally as "The Crop-Eared Flier." New York racing official and historian Walter S. Vosburgh declared Glenelg as the best three-year-old in the East and Herzog as the best in the West. The West, for New York racing men, then included Kentucky, Tennessee, and Ohio, where Herzog won six of seven races as a three-year-old, including the Cumberland Stakes at Nashville, Association Stakes at Louisville, the Phoenix Produce Stakes and Association Produce Stakes at Lexington, and two sweepstakes at Cincinnati, in one of which he lowered the world record for mile heats to 1:45 and 1:43 1/2. Western horsemen hailed Herzog as the best three-year-old since unbeaten Norfolk.

Success of Herzog came with happy timing, for it naturally increased the value of Dixie's subsequent foals, at a time when Major Thomas could use the money. His employers kept selling out from over him. For three years he was general manager of the Lexington *Observer and Reporter*, but lost this position when the paper was sold; for the next three years, he was a teller in the Farmers' and Traders' Bank of Lexington, but lost this job when the bank was sold. In 1870 his brother, as circuit judge, appointed Major Thomas as master commissioner for Fayette County, a position he relinquished soon after his brother's death. In 1874 he was elected sheriff and was reelected two years later, but by this time his relatively small horse breeding and racing operation was producing significant income and he decided to devote all his time to it.

In 1877 he purchased 250 acres on the Russell Cave Pike north of Lexington and named the farm Dixiana, in

59

honor of Herzog's dam. Iron gates at the entrance to Dixiana bore an inscription reflecting the owner's attitude toward traveling salesmen:

NOTHING EXCEPT

A GOOD

RACE HORSE

WANTED

*   *   *

AGENTS

FOR THE SALE OF

BOOKS, PATENT MEDICINES,

SEWING MACHINES,

AGRICULTURAL IMPLEMENTS,

HORTICULTURE &

NURSERY PRODUCTS AND

ESPECIALLY

OF LIGHTNING RODS

AND WIRE FENCES

NOT ADMITTED

*   *   *

VISITORS

OF EVERY NATIONALITY

WHO WILL COME UN TO MY HOUSE

ALWAYS WELCOME

*   *   *

B. G. THOMAS

Hira, the filly that refinanced Major Thomas's interest in racehorses after the war, was brought home after failing to win in her last five starts in New York during 1869. Her first two foals amounted to nothing, but her third, a bay colt by Alarm foaled in 1875, was special. According to an old story, whose improbability has failed to deter its perpetuation, Major Thomas asked one of his black grooms which of the two-year-olds appeared to be the best of the Dixiana horses in 1877. Pointing to Hira's Alarm colt, he responded, "Him yar."

Erudite Joe Palmer, who loved a neat story second only to the truth, suggested in the alternative that Himyar's name might reasonably have been derived from his first three dams. Himyar's third dam was Flight. His second dam was Hegira, an Arabian word meaning flight, with particular reference to Mohammed's flight from Mecca to Medina in the year 622. His first dam was Hira, former capital city of an Arabian kingdom long "one with Nineveh and Tyre," while Himyar was a ruler of Semitic people who inhabited a part of Arabia.

Be that as it may, Himyar was a good horse, "the greatest horse I ever bred," Major Thomas flatly declared, "indeed, Himyar was one of the greatest our Turf ever had." It should be noted that Major Thomas was selling hard, when so quoted. He had bred more celebrated racehorses than Himyar, such as Ban Fox, champion two-year-old of 1885; Correction, one of the fastest fillies New York had ever seen; and her full brother, Domino, universally recognized as America's greatest two-year-old and record money winner. But Major Thomas was standing Himyar at stud, selling services to him and yearlings by him, so it was not with complete objectivity that the "Nestor of the Turf," as he has come to be known in Kentucky, appraised Himyar in relation to horses of higher reputation he and others had bred.

Himyar lost his first start as a two-year-old in the spring of 1877, but was brought back in the fall at Lexington to win the six-furlong Colt Stakes over a heavy track by running "through his horses in fine style after a half-mile, and never being approached afterward, won as he pleased by nearly 20 lengths." Upon this one performance he was pronounced a phenomenon in Lexington. Three days later he won the mile Colt and Filly Stakes at Lexington, then won the Belle Meade Stakes at Louisville, before suffering an injury and finishing third in the Sanford Stakes. The next year as a three-year-old, Himyar began by winning the 1 1/2-mile Belle Meade Stakes at Nashville and ten days later won the 1 3/4-mile Phoenix

Hotel Stakes at Lexington under a strong pull. As a consequence, he was a 1–3 betting favorite for the fourth running of the Kentucky Derby at Louisville; he was backed heavily in the auction pools at Churchill Downs and caused something of a panic in every city where betting on the race was conducted, for he finished second to Day Star, which he had beaten often.

"There were all sorts of rumors," Vosburgh wrote years later, "one being that there was a combination to beat him. Besides his bad start, it was alleged that when he began over-hauling his field, one by one, some of the jockeys were heard to cry, 'Here he comes! Stop him!' and that they did all they could to impede him. Bob Swim was riding Leveller, and Swim's reputation as a foul rider was well known. There had been more money bet on Himyar in the 1878 Kentucky Derby than on any horse for years, and the temptation to 'stop' so great a favorite lent color to the charges."

Shipped to St. Louis, Himyar won at mile heats, then was returned to Lexington where he was started in September while not in form and was easily beaten at two-mile heats. As a four-year-old, he was undefeated in all four of his races. As a five-year-old, he won only four of a dozen races, beaten at times by indifferent horses, and he lost his only race at six. Thus over five racing seasons, Himyar won fourteen of twenty-seven races and earned $11,650, a record in which Major Thomas saw more than is readily apparent to others at this late stage.

By 1890 Major Thomas had cosigned more notes for friends than his friends could pay on, and it became necessary to sell Dixiana to Jacob S. Coxey (who later was to lead a civilian army on Washington). Major Thomas that year moved Himyar and his broodmare band to smaller acreage a mile west of Dixiana and named this place Hira Villa Stud, in honor of his mare Hira, the dam of Himyar, subsequent stakes winners Highflight and Sis Himyar, plus several high-priced racing prospects that did not turn out as well as their siblings. The best mare

Major Thomas ever owned did not have a name he could feel comfortable about hanging on the farm gate: Mannie Gray, by Enquirer. He bought her from his old commander, General Abe Buford, who had raced her as a three-year-old in 1877 to one spectacular victory. In the second race of her life, a six-furlong affair with a $150 purse at Lexington, Mannie Gray was entered in a large field of thirteen horses including H. Price McGrath's heavily favored Calvin, a half-brother to champion Tom Bowling, which two years earlier had won the Belmont Stakes and Jersey Derby. Mannie Gray ran off and hid from this field, winning by twenty lengths! General Buford ran her seven more times, at Louisville, Cincinnati, Lexington, and Nashville, and she never won another race.

For Major Thomas, however, Mannie Gray was a blue hen, a marvelous producer of an extraordinary number of stakes winners: Ten Strike, winner of the Tennessee Derby; Bandala, winner of the important Ladies Handicap in New York; Lady Reel, dam in turn of champion racehorse and leading sire Hamburg; Correction, also dam of Futurity winner Yankee; Freemason; and in 1891 at Hira Villa Stud, she foaled a colt by Himyar that was to be known as the Black Whirlwind.

This was Domino, a brilliant racehorse and a sire of lasting influence on the breed of American Thoroughbreds. Major Thomas sent Domino along with his other yearlings to be auctioned at Tattersall's annual sale at Seventh Avenue and Fifty-fifth Street in New York in 1892. Foxhall Keene saw him, liked him, and suggested to his father that he buy the colt. Multimillionaire James R. Keene, the Silver Fox of Wall Street who was just getting back into racing, thought the colt would command too high a price and did not bid on him; Foxhall bought him for $3,000, and he went into the Keene stable.

Born in London in 1838, James R. Keene came to America with his parents at the age of twelve and settled in San Francisco. He sold milk, worked in a mill, taught school, and edited a weekly newspaper. When he was thirty-five, he bought some mules and went into the hauling business, supplying the Bonanza mines in Nevada. He made $10,000 at this in one year, bought a seat on the San Francisco stock exchange, and in three years ran that stake into $6 million. He thereupon hired the first private car ever operated over the Union Pacific Railroad and moved to New York in style. A financial writer estimated Keene's Wall Street profits during his first two years in town to amount to $9 million.

At this time, the 1870s, tobaccomen Pierre and George Lorillard had emerged as dominant figures on the New York Turf, winning all the important fixtures, sometimes running 1-2-3. When Pierre's horses did not win, George's did. In 1878 the Lorillards had the best three-year-old colt in Duke of Magenta, the best three-year-old filly in Balance All, the best handicapper in Parole, and three of the year's best two-year-olds, Harold, Monitor, and Idler. Many New York owners believed the Lorillards would kill racing in New York unless someone could come up with a colt good enough to challenge Harold, Monitor, and Idler in the coming season's classic races. William Bathgate, a racing man in the brokerage house of Bathgate and Company, approached Keene with the idea that he buy Dan Swigert's good two-year-old, Spendthrift, which in five starts had proved that nothing in Kentucky or Tennessee could touch him; Keene bought him for $15,000. It was a good initial investment. For Keene, Spendthrift beat Lorillard horses in the 1879 Belmont Stakes, Champion, Jersey Derby, and Lorillard Stakes and was acclaimed the best three-year-old of the year. This hardly diminished the Lorillard supremacy, inasmuch as they raced the champion two-year-old colt in Sensation, champion two-year-old filly in Rosalie, and champion three-year-old filly in Ferida.

Keene was intrigued by the sport, however, and began investing in Kentucky yearlings and English broodmares. Pierre Lorillard also was enjoying great success on the

Major Barak G. Thomas, called the Nestor of the Turf (*Keeneland Library*)

James R. Keene, the Silver Fox of Wall Street, America's leading breeder and owner at the turn of the century

English Turf, his Iroquois in 1881 becoming the first American-bred to win the Epsom Derby as well as the classic St. Leger and five other stakes. Keene followed him to Europe with Spendthrift and a King Alfonso colt he named after his son, Foxhall. Spendthrift raced without success, but in 1881 Foxhall became the first American-bred to win the Grand Prix de Paris, and as an older horse won England's prestigious Ascot Gold Cup, and the Cesarewitch and Cambridgeshire handicaps. (Keene bet heavily on Foxhall, winning $360,000, and never bet on a horse again. He was said to have remarked, "Any man who bets consistently is a sucker.")

Keene shipped his English mares to Kentucky where one of them, bred to Spendthrift, produced Kingston. For other owners, Kingston established the present record for races won, eighty-nine; was at one time the world's leading money earner with $140,195; and twice led America's sire list. Kingston as a yearling and all the rest of Keene's horses were sold when Keene tapped out in the stock market.

Early in 1884 Keene entered into a plan with a few investors to corner the Chicago wheat market. He put $7.5 million into it and just missed; at a crucial moment, Chicago brokers refused to honor his certified checks. Keene hired a train and shipped bags of gold from New York to Chicago to handle the buying personally, but by the time he arrived, the corner had been broken. Jay Gould had been saying for some time, "Keene came East in a private car; I'm going to send him back in a box car." Gould applied pressure to Keene's stock market holdings and by the end of 1884, Keene not only had lost his fortune but also was $1.5 million in debt. Once powerful, courted, and feared, Keene for four years went "unnoticed, unsought, and regarded by the Street as an exploded bubble about to join the ranks of the vast army of Wall Street failures."

In the late 1880s, however, William Havemeyer asked Keene to handle the market operations of the sugar trust, and his business fortunes abruptly took an upward swing. Poor Keene was soon rich Keene, and by 1891 he started buying racehorses again. He asked his brother-in-law, Major Foxhall Daingerfield, to find a farm in Kentucky where he could breed some horses of his own. In 1893 Major Daingerfield picked out historic Castleton Farm on the Iron Works Pike, about six miles north of Lexington. This was the farm Virginian John Breckinridge had purchased in 1790 and called Cabell's Dale. It was John Breckinridge who drafted the Kentucky Resolutions, later embodied in the Virginia Resolutions. A United States senator, he served as attorney general in Thomas Jefferson's cabinet. His son Robert J. Breckinridge, a Princeton-educated lawyer, bred Thoroughbreds, became a Presbyterian minister, an anti-Catholic whose writings resulted in his being tried for heresy in Baltimore (acquitted), and ultimately president of Centre College in Danville. His daughter married John Castleman, who in 1840 built the Castleton mansion which still faces the Iron Works Pike and was one of the founders of the breed of American Saddle Horses. Castleman served as a captain under General John Hunt Morgan during the Civil War and rose to the rank of general in the Spanish-American War.

John C. Breckinridge, grandson of Jefferson's attorney general, lived in Lexington, was a United States senator, vice president under Buchanan, and the presidential nominee who split the vote that allowed Lincoln to enter the White House. As a major general, he commanded Kentucky's Orphan Brigade, later became secretary of war for the Confederacy. In addition to his duties as vice president of the United States, he served at the same time as president of the Kentucky Association race track in Lexington, a position he held until his death in 1875.

Under Keene's ownership and Major Daingerfield's management, Castleton Farm became the most prominent Thoroughbred breeding nursery in the world. From 1893 through 1912, there were foaled 113 stakes winners and an astounding succession of champions and leading sires bred or owned by Keene: Voter, Commando, Cap and Bells, Delhi, Sysonby, Peter Pan, Ballot, Colin, Celt, Ultimus, Maskette, Sweep, Black Toney, and Pennant. At the turn of the century, it seemed that the Turf had become Keene's private preserve. This was not completely true, for he had worthy adversaries: W. C. Whitney, August Belmont II, James Ben Ali Haggin, John E. Madden, John (Bet-a-Million) Gates, H. P. Whitney, and others. Keene beat them with regularity, for business and pleasure.

Keene's reentry in racing began with Domino, which he turned over to Albert Cooper to break as a yearling at the old Sheepshead Bay track on Long Island. Cooper tried Domino in the late fall of 1892 at a quarter-mile and he went so fast that Cooper would not believe his watch; so he sent Domino right back again for another quarter-mile and he ran it in the same time. This did two things: It convinced Cooper he had a very fast colt, and it caused Domino to bow both front tendons. When Domino was brought to the races the next year, he came in bandages.

Father and son merged their stables in 1893 and Domino was brought out for the first time at Gravesend on May 22, racing in the name of J. R. and F. P. Keene, trained by Billy Lakeland. Fred Taral, a Hall of Fame rider, whose contract had been purchased by the Keenes for $10,000, was up on Domino as in all but one of his starts; Taral was strong and he was a whip rider. As might be expected, Domino cared nothing for Taral as a rider, but apparently liked him for lunch, trying to bite him whenever possible. Foxhall Keene wrote that late in Domino's career, a blanket had to be thrown over his head before Taral could mount.

At any rate, Taral brought Domino down by six lengths in his first start, an overnighter, and five days later won the Great American Stakes by four lengths from Dobbins and Joe Ripley. In the Great Eclipse Stakes, he led throughout and "won easily by two lengths" from Dobbins and Declare. For the Great Trial Stakes two weeks later, Taral rode the Keenes' Hyder Abad, and Snapper Garrison rode Domino, leading all the way and winning by a neck from Hyder Abad, with Dobbins third.

Shipped to Chicago, Domino won the Hyde Park Stakes by two lengths from Peter the Great and Vassal, with a good horse, Rey El Santa Anita, fourth. A month later he was at Monmouth Park where he picked up the Produce Stakes with 128 pounds, beating Discount and Declare.

Ten days later, Domino was tested for the first time. This was the Futurity; with first money amounting to $48,910, it was the richest purse of the year and nineteen were going for it. Domino, carrying 130 pounds, got away in the second flight and almost fell over his stablemate, Hyder Abad, which went down in the mud, but got up to engage the leaders after a half-mile. Wrote the *Turf, Field and Farm* correspondent: "The leading bunch comprised Galilee, Dobbins, and Potentate in the order named. The latter was easily disposed of by Domino, who now, under Taral's most desperate drive, made play for the flying couple in advance, and catching up with them opposite the lower end of the grandstand, the last sixteenth furnished one of the most magnificent exhibitions of the kind ever witnessed. All the colts were dead game and stood punishment unflinchingly, while each of the three jockeys was riding as for dear life. Taral seemed to use superhuman efforts and finally landed Domino winner by a head." Galilee was second, Dobbins third.

First money in the Futurity raised Domino's earnings in seven starts to $145,980 and he thus became America's greatest money earner, surpassing Kingston's record of $140,195 earned with eighty-nine victories in 138 races. (With career earnings of $193,550, Domino reigned as America's leading earner longer than any other champion—twenty-seven years; his career mark was passed by

Man o' War in 1920. Domino's two-year-old earnings of $170,790 stood as a record for thirty-eight years, until surpassed by Top Flight in 1931.)

The Futurity marked the fourth time Domino had beaten Dobbins, but Richard (Boss) Croker, Dobbins's owner, still would not believe Domino was better than his horse. (Croker was a hard man to put down. Nearly everyone with him in Tammany Hall who was caught with a hand in the till was prosecuted, but not Croker; he took his cut and hied to Ireland. In 1907 he won the English Derby with Orby.) At any rate, a match race was run two days after the Futurity, same place, same distance, $10,000 a side, $2,500 added by the Coney Island Jockey Club.

For the first quarter-mile, Domino led Dobbins by a head, but for the next three furlongs, it seemed that Dobbins gained a slight lead. Then Domino came again and "they passed the post inseparably locked together." A dead heat was declared; the match and betting were declared off and no purse money was distributed.

Domino raced once more at two, winning the Matron Stakes at Morris Park and setting a new track record of 1:09 flat for the straight six furlongs.

In his first start at three, Domino ran his unbeaten streak to ten by winning the Withers Mile. In this race, he beat a top horse, Byron McClelland's Henry of Navarre, by a head; Domino never beat him again in four later meetings.

Eleven days later, Domino was in Chicago for the 1 1/2-mile American Derby. The Keenes figured Domino could carry his speed over a distance of ground if rated and Taral was so instructed; the pace was slow and Domino fought his rider for a mile and then when asked, had nothing. He finished ninth and last as E. J. (Lucky) Baldwin's Rey El Santa Anita picked up one of the four American Derbys won by Baldwin.

Foxhall Keene declared that Domino was lame and the colt was not raced for two months. He was brought back in the Flying Stakes, and he came down the Futurity Course at Sheepshead Bay virtually flying in 1:10 flat; he was carrying 130 pounds and this was the fastest the six furlongs had been run, but it was not the official record; Kingston held this (although it was known that he had been a member of a field which, by error, had been started from the 5 1/2-furlong post). Domino won the Ocean Handicap three days later, beat Clifford in a mile match race, then won the Culver Stakes, and four days later was drawn into a nine-furlong match race with Henry of Navarre.

The match race was a big event, drawing some 20,000 people to Brooklyn's Gravesend track; Domino was warmed up on the boulevard outside the track while Henry of Navarre was galloped twice around the track, then breezed an eighth of a mile, which is something not seen today. The start was quick, Domino taking a two-length lead; Sam Doggett let Henry of Navarre go at the half-mile pole and he caught Domino, getting his head in front at the head of the stretch. Domino fought back and the two went by the finish so close the judges could not separate them. It was declared a dead heat. Both horses were so tired that their owners decided to split the $5,000 purse rather than rerun the race.

A rematch was inevitable, however, and it came about three weeks later, with four-year-old Clifford added. Up to this time, Domino had lost only one race in his life, had beaten Henry of Navarre at a mile, had finished even with him after 1 1/8 miles, and had beaten Clifford at a mile; Clifford, champion three-year-old the previous season, had won nine of thirteen races at four and had beaten Henry of Navarre by a nose; Henry of Navarre had won the Belmont and Travers and had a string of ten consecutive victories going until Clifford beat him. This shaped up as an 1894 version of the Damascus–Buckpasser–Dr. Fager meeting in the 1967 Woodward Stakes.

Domino broke with his usual flash of speed. It carried him six furlongs. Henry of Navarre caught him and went by. Then Clifford came up and tried the leader, could not get by, and hung. Henry of Navarre won by three-quarters of a length. Domino reinjured a front foot and Taral brought him home, eleven lengths behind, seated flat on his saddle with a hand on his hip. It was Domino's last race at three.

At four, Domino won a six-furlong overnighter and then the Keenes, still thinking Domino could get a distance, sent him after the 1 1/4-mile Suburban with 123 pounds; he finished fourth. Three days later he won a 5 1/2-furlong overnighter, and four days after that he took up 130 pounds and won the six-furlong Coney Island Handicap. The next week he won the mile Sheepshead Bay Handicap with 127 pounds. It was his nineteenth and last victory.

Domino ran three more times. With 133 pounds, he failed by a head to give The Butterflies twenty-four pounds, finishing second in the Fall Handicap. In a special event at nine furlongs, he clung desperately to Henry of Navarre, but lost by a neck. Six days later, he raced his last, a 1 1/4-mile special event in which he was beaten after a mile and finished fifth to Henry of Navarre, Clifford, Sir Walter, and Rey El Santa Anita.

Retired to stud at Castleton Farm in Kentucky, Domino became and remains today one of America's most influential sires, which is odd, because he had little opportunity at stud. Good sires average about 300 foals. Among America's leading sires, Sir Gallahad III sired 567 foals, Blenheim II sired 530, and Star Shoot, 510. For a sire line to survive, it would seem imperative that it be characterized by quantity as well as quality. Yet Domino sired only nineteen named foals in two crops. His best son, champion racehorse and leading sire Commando, sired only twenty-seven named foals in four crops. As fountainheads go, this is just a trickle.

Nevertheless, the Domino-Commando male line, long characterized as a source of native speed, was represented by fifty-five descendants which won stakes during

72

1973. But for Domino there would have been no Commando, unbeaten Colin, Alsab, Ack Ack, Peter Pan, Black Toney, Double Jay, Spy Song, Crimson Satan, Bimlech, Blue Larkspur, Blue Swords, Market Wise, Pennant, Equipoise, Stymie, Carry Back. While these prominent racehorses and stallions descend from Domino directly in tail-male line, the influence of Domino in today's pedigrees is not restricted to just the top line of the pedigree; Domino's name appears elsewhere, in the middle of pedigrees as well, of more than 80 percent of all stakes winners in the United States today.

Domino died at Castleton on July 29, 1897, suffering from spinal meningitis, when the five foals in his first crop were sucklings. Of these five, three were to become stakes winners—Disguise, Doublet, and Runaway Girl (plus Pink Domino, dam of Sweep). Domino's second and last crop of fourteen foals included five stakes winners—Commando, Cap and Bells (first American-bred filly to win the English Oaks), Noonday (dam of five stakes winners including High Time), Olympian, Running Stream (dam of Ultimus), plus the dams of Theo Cook, Dominant, and Mystify. Thus from his nineteen progeny, Domino sired eight stakes winners—42 percent, as compared with the average of the breed, 2.5 percent stakes winners.

Domino was buried where he was foaled, at Hira Villa Stud. Some forty persons, including Major Thomas, attended the ceremonies. In Barre Granite with a Shamrock border is an inscription suggested by James R. Keene, simple truth not always found in things of this nature: "Here lies the fleetest runner the American Turf has ever known, and one of the gamest and most generous of horses."

LONGFELLOW

K ING OF THE TURF he was called. "Beyond question the most celebrated horse of the 1870s was Longfellow," declared historian Walter S. Vosburgh. "No horse of his day was a greater object of public notice. His entire career was sensational; people seemed to regard him as a super-horse."

Uncle John Harper was as old as the century when he sent his grand race mare, Nantura, two miles down the pike to General Abe Buford's Bosque Bonita Stud to be bred to "that English horse Buford's so high on," Leamington. Result of this mating was a big brown colt with a Roman nose accented by a wide blaze that ran over his nose. He was foaled at Harper's 2,400-acre Nantura Stud in Woodford County, Kentucky, on May 10, 1867, and in Uncle John's many years of raising and racing blooded horses, this one was his best.

He grew rapidly into one of the biggest colts in Kentucky, almost seventeen hands, so ungainly that no attempt was made to race him at two. During the peak of his fame in the East, a writer for the *Spirit of the Times* attempted to attach some literary significance to the King of the Turf and inquired of his owner if the colt were named after Henry Wadsworth Longfellow. "Never heared much of that feller," Uncle John remarked vague-

74

ly, "but that colt of mine's got the longest legs of any feller I ever seen."

Uncle John brought out Longfellow for the first time in Lexington in the spring of his three-year-old year for the Phoenix Hotel Stakes. He could not get out of his own way. General Buford also had a nice three-year-old from Leamington's first American crop by the name of Enquirer. In the first heat, Enquirer won easily in 1:44 3/4, with W. F. Stanhope's filly Catina finishing second and Longfellow third. In the second heat, Enquirer cantered home in 1:44 1/2 and Longfellow could not even beat the distance flag. Enquirer raced on unbeaten that season and was declared the champion three-year-old of 1870 after his victory in the Kenner Stakes at Saratoga. Uncle John took his big, green colt home to Nantura, turned him out to pasture, and when he brought him up in the fall, Longfellow was a different horse.

On September 16 at the Kentucky Association track in Lexington, Longfellow won the Produce Stakes, two-mile heats in 3:43 1/4 and 3:55 1/2, defeating John R. Viley's Twinkle and distancing H. T. Duncan's unnamed filly by Lexington–Ella D. Shipped to Cincinnati two weeks later, Longfellow won the Ohio Stakes in easy fashion, two-mile heats in 3:37 1/2 and 3:55 1/2, from Pilgrim, by Lexington, owned by Uncle John's neighbor, Dan Swigert, who had resigned the year before as manager of A. J. Alexander's Woodburn Stud.

Shipped to Nashville on October 12, Longfellow started in the Citizens' Stakes, two-mile heats, and lost the first heat to Lee Paul's Morgan Scout in 3:41 3/4, but came back in the second heat and distanced Morgan Scout and two other rivals. Two weeks later in Memphis, Longfellow closed out his three-year-old season with his fourth consecutive victory, winning the Post Stakes, two-mile heats in 3:40 1/4 and 3:40, defeating Defender (which he was to meet later), Morgan Scout, Mollie James, and Irene Sheppard.

Longfellow's autumn performances in the Midwest moved him up considerably in the opinion of many and he was considered to be among the ten best three-year-olds of the year, along with Enquirer, Kingfisher, Preakness, Telegram, Maggie B. B. (later to produce Iroquois), Remorseless, Lynchburg, Foster, and Kildare.

At four, Longfellow emerged as the best horse of the year. On May 24 in Lexington, nothing would oppose him and he was permitted to walk over for a $400 purse. He did not start again until July 5, when Uncle John shipped him east to old Monmouth Park for the second running of the Monmouth Cup at 2 1/2 miles. Helmbold, owned by William R. Babcock of Rhode Island, had won the inaugural Monmouth Cup and had been counted the champion handicapper the previous season. In addition to Helmbold, Milt Sanford's four-year-old Preakness and D. J. Crouse's four-year-old filly Regards also came out to test Longfellow. He won in a canter, covering the 2 1/2 miles in 4:41 1/4.

Nine days later Longfellow was at Saratoga and all except August Belmont's Kingfisher declined to run against him for the 2 1/4-mile Saratoga Cup. Charles Wheatly, starter for the race, said: "I shall never forget it. When the flag fell, Kingfisher shot away. As he did so, the big brown horse wheeled and gathered himself for a spring. He seemed to rise to an awful height, then he sprang forward, and in a twinkling he was in front." Longfellow turned in a 1:40 first mile and then finished off Kingfisher in facile fashion, with a final clocking in 4:02 3/4.

Victories in the Monmouth Cup and Saratoga Cup gave Longfellow the sobriquet of King of the Turf. Uncle John was ready to take his colt home, but was persuaded to stay on at Saratoga for the four-mile race the following month. In the interim, Longfellow walked over for an $800 purse.

On August 23, Longfellow was opposed by Helmbold again in the four-mile purse. A deluge hit the track the day before the race and turned it into a quagmire. Helmbold loved it, Longfellow did not, and Helmbold won easily.

Uncle John went home to tragedy. He was scheduled to race Longfellow in a match against Swigert's Pilgrim at the old Kentucky Association track on September 12. Rumors of prerace tampering prompted Uncle John to sleep at Longfellow's head in his barn in Lexington. Just before midnight on September 10, Uncle John was awakened by a stealthy rattle at the barn door.

"You can't come in here," Uncle John said, "go away." The door was gently tried again, but the visitor then mounted a horse and galloped away.

Early the next morning, news was brought from Woodford County that Uncle John's brother Jacob, 75, and their sister Betsy, 73, had been murdered in their small cottage on Nantura Stud.

Midway historian, J. A. Rogers, summarized this famous case in an account which appeared in the Lexington *Herald* of September 22, 1935:

Whether it was intended to kill old John Harper the same night that his aged brother and sister were murdered, is a part of the mystery of that terrible crime, but all the circumstances lead to the belief that it was the purpose of the assassin to include him in the slaughter. He was sleeping beside Longfellow at the track near Lexington that night—with his head almost touching the animal's flanks, the stable boys used to say—and was awakened at midnight by a stealthy rattle at the door. The horse was to run in a race of two-mile heats against Pilgrim the next afternoon, and there had been the usual rumors of intended assaults on the great racer. The old man shambled to the door and demanded the visitor's business. It was a disguised voice that answered: "I want to see Longfellow."

Uncle John was alone in the stable and the attendants sleeping overhead. "You can't come in here," he said. "Go away." The door was again gently tried by those on the outside and then rapid steps showed that the plot, whatever it was, had failed. Someone mounted a horse near by and galloped down the road. Early next morning news was brought in from Wood-

77

ford of the double murder at the Harper place. Jacob and Betsy Harper and old John lived alone in a dilapidated house, surrounded by one of the fairest farms in the world. Near the dwarfed old dwelling is a grove of large trees. In front are the stables, loosely put together of weather-beaten logs and boards. At a distance in the rear are the negro cabins. Some 2,400 acres of pasture and meadows stretch around on all sides. In the stables, the night of September 10, 1871, were a score of broodmares and blooded colts, and in the cabins slept 15 or 20 negroes. In the ramshackle old house, that night, there was believed to be no one but the aged brother and sister of John Harper when the doors were locked at 9 o'clock.

Before daylight the next morning two of the servants came to the house to get breakfast. Their repeated knocks were not answered. They tried the doors and windows and found them securely fastened. They shouted loudly to the old people, but there was no response. At last they broke open a door with an ax. It was a bloody story that the first hurried search of the frightened negroes told. In one of the rooms Jacob Harper, 75 years old, was found dead, his head beaten to a shapeless mass. On the white pillow was the still fresh red imprint of a hatchet. The old man had striven to rise and one foot touched the floor, but it was clear that the murderer had forced him back upon the bed, and then had finished his bloody work. In the adjoining room Betsy Harper, two years younger than her brother, was still breathing feebly, but across her forehead were five ugly gashes. She died two days later, having spoken but twice. Once she said: "It must have been some of our own."

In an outhouse the hatchet was found, covered with blood, but the murderer had left no other trace of the methods or purpose of his crime. The house had not been ransacked, although the murderer had plenty of time and was secure from interruption. Only a trifle of loose change that Jacob Harper carried was taken and thousands of dollars in bonds and money was left behind untouched. It was very certain that the object was not plunder. The old people were singularly inoffensive, having but little to do with their neighbors; nor could it be found that they had had any quarrel with a servant. How entrance was gained into the house was never learned, but fresh tracks leading to a spot where two horses had stood, showed how the escape was made.

White panel fences slashing through Bluegrass pastures have identified Kentucky Thoroughbred nurseries, such as Calumet Farm, for more than a half-century. (© *Tony Leonard*)

Counted a phenomenon as a two-year-old, Domino proved to be a foundation sire of speed. A marker over his grave is inscribed: "Here lies the fleetest runner the American Turf has ever known, and one of the gamest and most generous of horses."

(From a painting by A. H. Pease)

A record crowd of 163,628 persons attended the 100th running of the Kentucky Derby at Churchill Downs in Louisville. The purse for the 1975 running won by Foolish Pleasure amounted to $262,100.

(© *Tony Leonard*)

Lexington, America's leading sire for an unprecedented sixteen years, was bred in 1850 by Dr. Elisha Warfield, Father of the Kentucky Turf, and stood at R. A. Alexander's Woodburn Stud in Woodford County. His skeleton now is on display in the Smithsonian Institution in Washington.

(From a painting by Edward Troye)

Racing as it was meant to be is conducted at Keeneland during short, three-week meetings in the spring and fall. Breeders, owners, trainers, jockeys, and racing fans are close to horses in the Keeneland paddock. (© *Tony Leonard*)

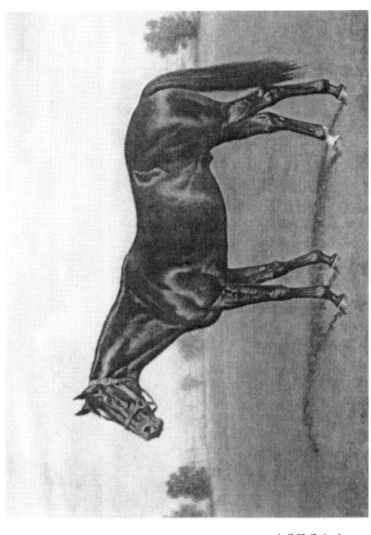

America's most successful native stallion of this century, Bold Ruler sired eighty stakes winners while standing at Claiborne Farm near Paris, Kentucky.

(From a painting by Richard Stone Reeves, Oxmoor House, Birmingham, Alabama)

Syndicated Secretariat romps in his paddock at Claiborne Farm near Paris, Kentucky, where his noted sire, Bold Ruler, was raised and stood. (© *Tony Leonard*)

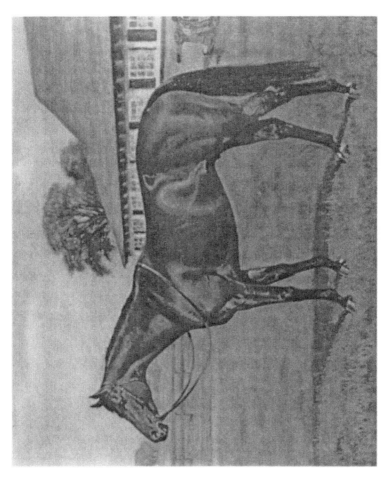

Greatest of the many top runners bred by Warren Wright at Calumet Farm was champion Citation, which set a world record for the mile and was the first horse to earn more than a million dollars in purses.

(From a painting by F. B. Voss)

Longfellow won his race that day. For the first time, his master was not by to watch the start, to follow his favorite with anxious eyes around the course and to blanket him as he was led to the stable. As the noble beast came in a winner at the Lexington course, the body of his master's brother, without religious exercises of any kind, was carried to his grave, in a corner of the Harper farm, 14 miles away from the race meeting. Then John Harper set himself to the work of finding the murderer. He offered a reward of $5,000 for his apprehension, and a famous detective from Covington came down to the farm. Within three days he gave up the case after an interview with the old man. It was rumored at the time that he took the $5,000 with him, but to the people around about there seemed to have been found no clew.

Longfellow's grand achievement at Saratoga, the summer before, was still the boast of every Kentuckian, and his master was included in the pride that Kentucky had in the horse. So, when it was reported that an intended assault had been made upon the old man on the night of the double murder, the neighborhood was aroused as it had never been over a similar crime. Suspicion fell upon the negroes on the place. Two of them were suspected, an old colored woman and a young boy. Three nights after the murder a band of disguised men knocked at the doors of the two cabins. The purpose of their visit was not doubted, but no resistance was offered. It was not so long after the war that the dignity and power of the law had reasserted itself in Kentucky. Crime was terribly frequent in all parts of the state and Judge Lynch held frequent court. So there was huddling together of the frightened negroes on the night of this visit and perhaps some uncertainty as to which were the victims to be chosen. Few words were spoken as the woman and boy were taken from their beds, except that the woman shrieked and pleaded for mercy. The boy stolidly accepted his fate—so the whispered reports of that night's events afterward said. The two were bound together and the other end of the rope was caught by a man well masked and on horse back, as the hurried march to the neighboring wood was begun. What were the thoughts, the sufferings, of those two helpless creatures on their way can not be told, but the woman did not cease to protest her innocence of any crime. When charged with the murder of the master and mistress—they were then under a low branched tree—both fell

79

on their knees, and, with hands raised to the heavens that were black with the darkness of night, they solemnly declared that they were guiltless. Little shrift was given them. For the credit of man, let it be hoped that their crime seemed proved; at least the awful shame of that night was at the last tempered with a grain of mercy. The woman and the boy were both hanged until death was so near that when cut down by a repentant hand, they lay upon the ground gasping and senseless. With returning consciousness they still declared their innocence, and this time they were believed. The murderer of the aged brother and sister still goes unpunished, but no man in Kentucky today will excuse the act that so nearly added a greater crime to that which it was intended to avenge.

Of heirs to the fortune of the Harpers there were many in Woodford and the neighboring counties. The two brothers and the sister had mutually agreed—neither being married—that to the survivor should go the portions of the others. With the death of the last of the three, in default of a will, the estate was to be divided among the kin. Hence, conjecture found room for suspicion in the apparent attempt to make way with the two brothers and the sister on the same night. It was found that the time between the murder at the Harper house and the visit of the stranger at the door of Longfellow's stable, 14 miles away, just allowed for a rapid gallop from the one point to the other. The sound of galloping horses' hoofs was heard all along the road from the Harper farm to the Lexington racetrack, between 10 o'clock and 12 that night.

However unjustly, this suspicion grew to point to Adam Harper, a nephew of the three old people and one of the nearest beneficiaries through their death. Adam Harper demanded an investigation and the grand jury failed to return an indictment upon the evidence presented. Wallace Harper, a cousin, charged that Adam was involved in the murder and Adam promptly filed a $500,000 slander suit against Wallace. The trial, transferred from Woodford County to neighboring Scott County, was distinguished by the prominence of attorneys for both sides.

Representing the plaintiff were Thomas Payne Porter, former Lieutenant Governor of Kentucky; Andrew Jackson James, former Attorney General and Secretary of State for Kentucky; and Alvin Duvall, former judge of the Court of Appeals and of

80

Champion Longfellow
and his owner-breeder,
John Harper of
Midway, Kentucky

the Scott Circuit Court. Among counsel for the defendant were young Jo. C. S. Blackburn, then a member of the Kentucky legislature who was to serve in the House of Representatives and Senate for 32 years, from 1875 until his appointment as governor of Panama; and James E. Cantrill, who was to be elected Lieutenant Governor, judge of the Scott Circuit Court, and judge of the Court of Appeals.

The first count in the petition of the plaintiff charged his relative with saying that Adam and John W. Harper, his son, were at the head of the murder of Jacob and Betsy Harper. The defendant denied using the specific language charged, asserting that he had said: "From all the circumstances surrounding and connected with the killing, I am compelled to believe the said Adam guilty, and will continue so to believe until his innocence is proven; and further, that all his neighbors believe the same." The testimony introduced by the defense was simply to prove justification for the alleged libel. A detective swore that the tracks leading from the Harper house after the murder, exactly fitted the boots worn by Adam Harper and his son. The motive for the murder was sought to be shown in the proof that Adam Harper was in exceedingly straitened circumstances at the time, but he boasted of expecting soon to come into a large sum of money; while this was impossible, except upon the expectation of receiving property from an outside source. The murder was done with an old hatchet which, lost for a year or more before, had been found the day previous to the crime, and had been seen by Adam Harper then. When the relatives and neighbors gathered at the house on the morning after the murder, Adam Harper picked up this hatchet, and, with apparent irrelevancy, insisted upon showing to the bystanders that the murder must have been done by a right-handed man. Adam Harper was left-handed. It was also sought to be proven that Adam Harper was foremost among those who brought about the lynching of the innocent negroes.

On the part of the plaintiff it was proven that, before Betsy Harper's death, she saw him more than once, and did not declare his guilt, although she was in possession of all her faculties, and being asked by a neighbor who had done the deed, she answered: "I do not know."

The jury brought in a verdict for the defendant and afterward John Harper, the plaintiff's son, attempted to shoot Capt. Blackburn, the young lawyer who had been most conspicuous among the counsel in the effort to prove Adam Harper guilty of murder. The weapon was diverted, however, by a bystander, and the life of the future congressman saved. Adam Harper again presented himself before a grand jury for examination upon the evidence brought out in this trial, but although the feeling against him was so intense in his county that a change of venue had been granted him in the libel suit because of the manifest prejudice against him, the bill was again rejected, being supported by no satisfactory proof.

It is said that old John Harper never recovered from the terrible shock of that night, and from the revelation that was made to him by the Covington detective. He was always a silent man, little given to cheerful ways or to the companionship of any creature except his beloved horse: But those who saw him at Long Branch in the summer of 1872 noticed that Longfellow's victory over Harry Bassett did not arouse that exultation in the old man that the splendid performances of his great horse had done at Saratoga the year before; and, when the horse came in disabled, with Harry Bassett in the lead, two weeks later, John Harper's heart was broken. When he died in 1874, in the house that had such terrible associations for him, he left a will naming Frank Harper, another nephew, as his heir. Adam Harper still lived in Woodford county, a poor man.

At any rate, Longfellow easily won his rematch with Pilgrim (which he had beaten in the Ohio Stakes the previous year), two-mile heats in 3:38 3/4 and 3:41 1/4, and then was turned out at Nantura. A writer for the *Spirit* visited Nantura, interviewing Uncle John in the morbid atmosphere of the cottage, and asked if Longfellow would race again. A new, younger star had risen in the East, Colonel David McDaniel's Harry Bassett, which had lost his first start, then won three races at two and all nine of his races at three, including the Belmont, Jersey Derby, Travers, Kenner, Champion, Reunion, and Bowie stakes (defeating Helmbold). The reporter asked Uncle John if Longfellow could handle Harry Bassett. "I'm agoing to have Longfellow in a fix to run next year," he told the

Spirit's man, "and when I get him ready, I'm agoing to fetch him East; then you'll see what he kin do."

Longfellow's preparation at five began at Lexington on May 15 in a 1 1/2-mile purse race which he won in a canter in 2:41 1/4 from two fillies. Three days later he won the three-mile Wooley Stakes by eight lengths in 6:00 3/4, beating J. W. Hunt Reynolds's Metella, Major Barak Thomas's Talaria, H. P. McGrath's Susan Ann, and General Buford's Hollywood. In both races, Longfellow was left out of the betting pools.

Meanwhile, Harry Bassett had begun his four-year-old season by defeating Longfellow's good stablemate Lyttleton in the 2 1/4-mile Westchester Cup on June 8 at Jerome Park and three days later had distanced Reynolds's mare Metella in a purse race, extending his winning streak over three seasons to fourteen.

Clamor rose for a match between the two best horses in training, Longfellow from the West, Harry Bassett from the East.

Uncle John shipped Longfellow east in a special railroad car bedecked with a banner: "LONGFELLOW ON HIS WAY TO MEET HIS FRIEND HARRY BASSETT IN THE MONMOUTH CUP." In 1949 Eddie Read drummed up some hot publicity around Your Host's coming to the Kentucky Derby from California, but the only comparable build-up for an intersectional meeting since Harry Bassett–Longfellow was the 1955 match of Swaps and Nashua.

On July 2, 1872, the long-awaited meeting took place at Long Branch, New Jersey. Harry Bassett was favored. But as with the Swaps–Nashua match eighty-three years later, Longfellow won in such an easy manner as to throw suspicion on the fairness of the contest. Harry Bassett went with Longfellow for only a short way, "sulked after a mile and a half and the race was over, Longfellow galloping in alone." Longfellow's winning margin was estimated at 100 yards; his time for the 2 1/2 miles was 4:34—good, but unspectacular.

Two days later Longfellow was brought out for the Jersey Jockey Club Purse, best three-out-of-five mile heats and was left out of the betting pools. He won in progressively faster times, 1:56 1/4, 1:54, and 1:43 3/4, over McGrath's Susan Ann, Reynolds's Metella (which was making a career out of chasing Longfellow), and A. C. Franklin's Arizona.

Harry Bassett was shipped to Saratoga and on July 13 he beat Lyttleton again in a prep race for the return meeting three days later with Longfellow in the 2 1/4-mile Saratoga Cup. Longfellow was heavily favored this time, $775 in the pools to $250 for Harry Bassett, with $20 buying a chance on Defender, owned by John Morrissey.

Going to the post, Longfellow struck the quarter of his left forefoot and twisted his racing plate. At the start of the race, Harry Bassett took the track with Longfellow in close pursuit. Rounding the first turn, it was apparent that something was wrong with Longfellow. He faltered and Harry Bassett drew off. Longfellow's rider, Joe Colston, went to the whip, the first such call the gallant racer ever had known. He answered with the finest resolution and closed the gap separating him from the fleeing Harry Bassett; he lurched, wobbled in his stride, but struggled on. Still answering the call of his rider, Longfellow forced Harry Bassett (in receipt of six pounds) to the very last ounce of strength to maintain a length advantage at the finish. The winning time was 3:59, the fastest 2 1/4 miles ever raced up to that time.

Longfellow was through. He limped back to the judges' stand, "his progress marked by only three hoofprints." His front left foot had been mutilated; a twisted shoe had been bent double during the race and was embedded in the frog of the foot. Longfellow could not bear the pain of the foot's touching the track.

Uncle John, with tears streaming down his old cheeks, tenderly draped a blanket over the back of his valiant horse. "I'm taking him home," he said softly, and the old man, supported by his cane, led off his limping champion. There were no cheers for Harry Bassett.

At stud, Longfellow proved to be highly successful, becoming America's leading sire in 1891 when his progeny earned $168,840 that season. He sired at least forty-two stakes winners, four of which were champions: The Bard, Freeland, Longstreet, and Thora. Other distinguished stakes winners by Longfellow were Kentucky Derby winners Leonatus and Riley, Oaks winners Dare Vela, Florimore, Kaloolah, Lavine Belle, Longitude, and United, plus such as Bill Letcher, Leonard, Long Dance, Long Taw, Longview, Nahma, Rainbow, all winners of major fixtures in the United States, in addition to Passaic, winner of the City and Suburban Handicap in England.

On November 5, 1893, Longfellow died, and Frank Harper had a stone shaft placed over his grave. A similar one is over the adjacent grave of Ten Broeck, and the oldest equine markers in Central Kentucky may be seen today in a small cemetery near Midway, on land once a part of Nantura Stud. Moss clings to the inscription:

LONGFELLOW
King of Racers
and
King of Stallions

HAMBURG

Y̶OUNG MAN, do you own that colt?"

"That depends on whether you want to buy him or attach him," replied John E. Madden.

The stranger was thinking about buying. He clasped his hands behind his back and circled the horse, studying the colt which had just accomplished what no other two-year-old in Turf history had managed, carrying a monstrous burden of 135 pounds to victory in the important Great Eastern Stakes.

"What's your price?"

Madden was preoccupied, checking his colt for cuts, feeling his ankles for heat, which might indicate a serious injury. "Fifty thousand dollars," he said over his shoulder and continued his careful inspection.

"Hmmmm," said the stranger, for this was 1897, and the highest price ever paid for a racehorse in training was $40,000, a sum paid thirty-three years earlier when millionaire Leonard Jerome purchased champion Kentucky as a sire prospect.

There was more circling, some casual counteroffers, and more hmmmms. Madden was a horse trader; he owned none that he was not ready to sell—at his price. The stranger finally offered $40,000, and Madden seemed tempted, but then shook his head, as though he just could not bring himself to let go of such a marvelous horse for mere money.

The stranger thereupon wrote out a Wells-Fargo draft for $40,000, took a silver dollar from his vest pocket, and flipped it into the air. Madden caught the coin and the deal was made, at $40,001.

Subject of the trade was Hamburg, which horsemen were calling a better two-year-old than brilliant Domino. Purchaser of Hamburg was copper king Marcus Daly, to whom money was a burden. The seller was America's greatest professional horseman.

This is legend. As with most legends, it is partly true. It is one of many that grew around the extraordinary person of John E. Madden. As a rule, one should not tamper with legends, but the simple facts relating to this man's phenomenal success with Kentucky horses are every bit as interesting as the fanciful tales in which he actually took no part.

For example, he was not John L. Sullivan's sparring partner. While said to be a veteran of some two hundred ring encounters, Madden flatly denied ever having fought professionally. As a youth in Pennsylvania, he was one of those who could be counted on to emerge from the crowd to challenge the bareknuckle fighter who was part of every county fair; by staying three minutes, he would pick up in side bets $100 or so, which invariably was invested in a horse. In later years, when Madden's horse investments totaled more than a million dollars, his friend Gentleman Jim Corbett, who took the title from Sullivan, was a guest at Hamburg Place and may have given an exhibition of his footwork in Madden's well-appointed gymnasium at the farm. A former featherweight champion, Billy Murphy, was hired by Madden to give boxing instructions to his sons.

In the days when Sullivan was chopping wood on the vaudeville circuit and challenging everybody in the bar, Madden won a race with a trotter that cost some betting sharks a good deal of money; they set upon him in the barn area and apparently drew some blood. Madden returned to his hotel, washed, and changed his clothes. In the lobby he encountered some friends of his latest adversary and suggested he still thought he could beat the man if given a fair show. This perked interest, particularly when Madden offered to bet the $200 purse he had won in the race. A match was quickly arranged, a ring set up in a stable.

According to a newspaper account, "When the men faced each other, Madden's antagonist was stripped to the waist and full of confidence. Madden turned up his coat collar, walked up to the 'rough guy' and lambasted him all over the barn. In five minutes he was master of the situation, collected $400, and quietly returned to the hotel. He was never challenged again by anyone in that gang." It is easy to see how from this startling reversal of form, a legend could emerge that Madden could handle even the mighty John L. when the money was down.

While in his teens, Madden was a champion runner, claiming all Pennsylvania records from 100 yards to five miles, but he had never beat a Thoroughbred in a match race. At the age of fifty-one, he almost did it.

"John Madden was the performer of an athletic feat at the Brighton Beach track yesterday," reported the *New York Herald* of July 18, 1907, "which not alone prevented possible fatalities, but aroused much admiring comment on the perfect physical control of the noted Kentucky horseman. He had left his horse and buggy tied to a rail in the paddock. Flies caused the horse much irritation and finally, in tossing his head, the animal broke loose from the railing and started to run in the direction of the gate, through which at that hour hundreds of women and men were entering the course.

"Madden, who was talking with Francis R. Hitchcock, looked up, saw the danger, and in a dozen gigantic bounds he had overtaken the horse, threw his arms around the animal's neck—the bridle having slipped off when the animal bolted—and within a few yards had brought the horse to a standstill, using the well-known method of squeezing the horse's nostrils so that he could not breathe. 'I have not a medal with me,' said Mr. Hitchcock, 'But I'll see that you receive one, John.' Hundreds of horsemen in the paddock when yesterday's feat was achieved said that they had never seen a circus act done with such confidence."

Madden prided himself in his physical fitness; he had a tendency to vault high plank fences when showing visitors his yearlings at Hamburg Place, liked to jog the mile from his cottage to Sheepshead Bay when training his horses in New York, never smoked, prohibited his farm employees from drinking Coca-Cola, said he swam in the spring-fed pond he had walled at the farm every day of the year he was in Lexington, and once was observed by a reporter negotiating the steeplechase course at Saratoga early one morning. Such things, when attributed to a millionaire in his fifties, are the stuff of legends.

John E. Madden was a complex man who revealed no more to his contemporaries than he chose, leaving contradictory impressions, but we can set down some of his accomplishments, from which one can gain an impression of the Thoroughbred racing and breeding industry as it emerged from the nineteenth century.

Patrick Madden, an Irish immigrant employed in the zinc works in Bethlehem, Pennsylvania, died in 1860, leaving a widow, three small children, and precious few worldly goods. At three years of age, John E. Madden's inheritance consisted of an alert mind and sound body, ambition and necessity; with these, he made a fortune. He grew up in the hard, dreary, coal and steel region of Pennsylvania whose by-product was hard young men singularly suited for athletics. Young Madden grew quickly to within a half-inch of six feet, with 180 pounds well proportioned over a powerful frame; he became a champion runner and high jumper, captained the Bethlehem East End baseball team, and loved boxing best of all. It was his athletic abilities that gave him his start in the horse business.

At county fairs, Madden set his foot-racing records, putting on exhibitions between trotting races. It was not long before he was riding, rather than running, around these tracks; he drove and won trotting races before he was sixteen years of age, collecting enough fees to buy his own trotter, which he traded for another. Traveling from one fair to another, Madden continued to trade, by his account getting better horses all the time. Side bets on foot races and boxing exhibitions provided boot for trading up; with better horses to drive, he won more races and bigger wagers. By the time he was twenty-eight, his success was such that he could trade for a good trotter, a gray gelding named Class Leader which he raced to a 2:22 1/4 record at a Grand Circuit meeting in Cleveland. Class Leader was Madden's first name horse and, for the two seasons he campaigned him (sharing sleeping quarters in a stall), his only horse.

High-wheel drivers then were singing the praises of the Belmont–Waterwitch pedigree cross. Madden listened. He remembered a stallion by Belmont out of Waterwitch which had been exported to England; he gambled on the success of the trip, bought the stallion for $4,000, brought him back to America, stood him for six months, and sold him to Samuel Browne and Senator Stockbridge for $15,000. It was his first big horse deal. He decided to move his base of operation to the Phoenix Hotel in Lexington, Kentucky.

"When I left Bethlehem, Pa.," he said later, "my chief stock in trade was pride and a few good trotting horses." He had more than that when he showed up in Kentucky at the age of thirty. He had a keen eye for a horse and a burgeoning reputation as a shrewd dealer in high-priced trotters. He bought at good prices and resold at fancier prices such noted Standardbreds as Suisun, 2:18 1/2;

Rachel B., 2:18 1/4; Belle Vara, 2:08 3/4; Wyandotte, 2:24 1/2; Abbie V., 2:16 3/4; and the noted stallion Robert McGregor, 2:17 1/2.

As a matter of court record, when Madden came to Kentucky, "he was engaged in raising, training, and driving trotting horses and had accumulated by reason of his energy, skill, and labor, and owned in his own right more than $150,000." This was a great deal of money at that time, and he had made it the hard way—on his own.

Madden was a loner. He gambled that his judgment of a horse was better than that of older horsemen; it was a precarious road to success, for one early error of judgment can terminate the journey. Those who successfully travel this route often are hard, shrewd men, self-confident, unemotional, suspicious, and eventually lonely. During his long career, Madden had many partnerships and associations, but basically, Madden was in business for himself. He played his hand against the world.

A trotting-horse man in the Bluegrass of Kentucky is not in the majority. Although there were many prominent Standardbred breeders in the vicinity, a man desiring to talk horse very long in Lexington eventually must concern himself with Thoroughbreds. This was no problem for Madden. He was capable of dealing in high-priced horses of any breed. During the 1890s Madden heard rumors in the trotting world that indicated to him the trotting business was verging on the slows; at the same time, the Thoroughbred business seemed to be improving, revitalized by a new racing administration in New York.

Immediately after the Civil War, wealthy New Yorkers such as Leonard Jerome, August Belmont I, William R. Travers, James Gordon Bennett, Pierre Lorillard, and William H. Vanderbilt organized fashionable racing clubs which conducted high-society meetings at Jerome Park, Saratoga, and Monmouth Park. Before the Civil War, racing was centered largely in the South, short meetings, heat races for $300 purses, a sport that commanded widespread interest and considerable sectional fervor. This southern sport survived Appomattox only in Kentucky.

A new game with different patrons began when Jerome Park was opened in New York in 1866. Heat racing was replaced by dash racing, six races with different horses each day; meetings extended beyond a week; purse money offered by the affluent clubs became significant; wagering became more widespread with the introduction of professional stakeholders, soon to be known as book-makers. The most significant change in New York racing, however, was a newfound respectability brought to it by the interest and involvement of wealthy, socially prominent men. Like tennis a century later, horse racing became a fad of New York society, as topical as the Metropolitan Opera, for both gentlemen and ladies. The fad lasted for little more than a decade.

By 1890 the gambling element predominated racing. Jerome, Travers, and Belmont died; Lorillard dispersed his stable. The tracks and races were controlled by book-makers. Tracks competed with concurrent meetings. The sport took on an unsavory flavor. An attempt was made to bring some sort of order out of the chaos with the formation of the Board of Control, made up of four representatives of track owners and three representatives of horse owners, but this proved to be a board with no control. Racing became a public nuisance and in 1893 was outlawed in New Jersey, while a constitutional convention in New York passed what apparently was intended as a similar prohibition.

Test court cases seemed to indicate that oral wagers, with no books and ledgers maintained, were not within the constitutional prohibition of gambling, and racing was continued in New York, ostensibly under a form of government control through an agency called the Racing Commission, whose chairman was August Belmont II. In 1894 The Jockey Club was formed in New York by fifty wealthy men; the club promulgated racing rules, issued licenses for persons to participate in racing in New York, appointed judges, and allocated nonconflicting racing dates for Sheepshead Bay, Brighton Beach, Gravesend, Morris Park, and Saratoga race meetings, all with the blessing of the Racing Commission. The Jockey Club also purchased the *American Stud Book*, the first six volumes of which had been published by Colonel Sanders D. Bruce. With the purchase of the stud book, The Jockey Club became the registrar of all Thoroughbreds in America. Thus with the vesting of self-discipline in The Jockey Club, some rule and order emerged, integrity of Thoroughbred pedigrees was enhanced, chicanery was reduced with the exclusion of undesirable persons, and racing in New York donned a new respectability and stability.

John E. Madden noticed this. Harness racing, dispersed throughout the Midwest with no central governing body such as The Jockey Club, did not appear to have the potential for economic growth that he envisioned for Thoroughbred racing and breeding. He made a practice of going where the money was, and he gradually shifted his attention to Thoroughbreds, lessening but never divesting himself of his interests in Standardbreds. In 1890 he brought out his trotter Suisun to win the Clay Stakes at Albany, New York, and a week later his two-year-old Thoroughbred Dundee beat Ida Pickwick (later to be known as the Queen of the West, victress in forty-four races) in the Great Western Stakes at St. Louis.

In the Gay Nineties, the listing of horse owners was more casual than it is today. One horse might be involved in successive part sales and concurrent ownership, and several men might claim it as his horse, while published race summaries would simply list the trainer of the horse as its owner. In addition to the Great Western, Dundee won the Turf Exchange Stakes, Gaston Hotel Stakes, and Sandford Stakes that season in the name of Umbrella McGuigan, a Lexington horseman forever wary of rain.

Madden also raced Thoroughbreds in the name of Gus Straus, a Lexington merchant whose name became an integral part of the patois of the Turf by reason of its adorning a Main Street building: To dismiss a horse as having no chance in a race, old Kentucky horsemen would say, "He couldn't beat a fat man from here to the Straus Building."

The first good Thoroughbred Madden shipped to New York was Harry Reed, which raced in Straus's name. Madden bought Harry Reed as a yearling in Lexington for $400, broke him at Churchill Downs, and shipped him to New York in May of 1894 where he won his first start by three lengths. Two weeks later Harry Reed won the Van Nest Stakes and Madden promptly sold him for $10,000 to Mike Dwyer. Madden had been doing this sort of thing with Standardbreds for a while—running $400 up to $10,000 with about eight months of training—but this was the first time with a Thoroughbred.

Something should be said here about Mike Dwyer. He and his brother Phil were the leading Turfmen in America from the time they raced their first champion, Vigil, in 1876 until they dissolved their partnership in 1890; their colors were carried by an extraordinary succession of champions—Bramble, Luke Blackburn, Hindoo, Miss Woodford, Hanover, Kingston, Tremont, Runnymede, George Kinney, Inspector B., Sir Dixon, Dewdrop, and Bella B. Mike was a heavy bettor, an insatiable bettor—he would wager $30,000 to win $5,000, and often lost, a habit that irritated and embarrassed his brother and ultimately led to dissolution of their partnership.

At any rate, by 1894 Mike Dwyer was busy introducing Richard (Boss) Croker to the joys of this game. Croker had skimmed so much money through Tammany Hall that Mike could not get it all down with bookmakers in New York. At about the same time, a troublesome investigation into New York's vast political corruption dictated Croker's immediate departure from the country. Dwyer thought the timing neat. He and Croker, together with Dwyer's new speed horse, Harry Reed, shipped to England with a grand design to wipe out the entire British betting system with one deft blow. This was not so much a case of one's reach exceeding his grasp, for John Gates had grasped a nickname, Bet-a-Million, and considerable increment to his barb-wire and oil fortune with successful forays into British betting circles. Dwyer, however, had lost his touch. On the appointed day, Harry Reed dwelt at the start, and Dwyer dropped $240,000. While this misadventure did not trouble Croker (he was to buy a castle in Ireland, breed an English Derby winner, and never go to jail), Dwyer returned home a broken man. He never lost his enthusiasm for the big wager, just the means to participate. Thereafter, he reduced his play and was said to have dropped only $5,000 in 1897, when his heavily favored four-year-old champion, Ben Brush, suffered a stunning upset, losing by a nose to an unheralded two-year-old, a proper 40–1 shot named Plaudit, owned and trained by John E. Madden.

Another nice horse Madden raced in Straus's name was Amanda V, which in the spring of 1895 won the Pepper Stakes and La Belle Stud Stakes in Lexington and the Debutante Stakes in Louisville. She was by Strathmore out of Lady Reel, a half-sister to mighty Domino, and probably was the reason Madden that fall was to go back to the same well, Lady Reel; he bought her weanling colt, by Hanover, for $1,200 from Con Enright of Elmendorf Farm near Lexington. Madden named the colt Hamburg.

Hamburg was the hardest yearling Madden said he ever had to break. He could not get an exercise boy to stay on him. Hamburg lost a good deal of his mane, for riders kept taking handfuls with them as they went off. Madden finally borrowed from Major Barak Thomas a boy who could stay with the colt. According to Hiram Steele, who was Madden's foreman for many years, Hamburg as a yearling was breezed on six consecutive days, "and on the sixth day he went three furlongs in :35." This is hard to believe, for no one works yearlings so hard and often today, but many things attributed to good horses developed by Madden are hard to believe. Madden said Hamburg ate so much he required twice the work of average horses.

Increased work apparently increased Hamburg's appetite; he ate and worked, and ate and worked, and on June 7, 1897, at Gravesend in New York, Madden brought out a marvelously muscled two-year-old with a large blaze and hind white stockings which broke so fast there was suspicion of a false start. He won easily; four days later he won again by three lengths. Then he finished third to Bowling Brook. Two weeks later, however, Hamburg beat Bowling Brook easily, galloping home by four lengths in the important Great Trial Stakes, worth $16,550. This purse is not impressive today when pari-mutuel wagering and television rights can provide a pot of $350,000 for a match race, but in 1897 the Great Trial was the third richest race of the year (the Futurity was worth $34,290, the Realization, $18,125; no other race was worth as much as $10,000).

Five days later, Hamburg won the Double Event Stakes with the onerous burden of 129 pounds. Standard weight for a two-year-old was 122, one pound or two pounds additional being counted significant enough to cause a horse to win or lose a race. Yet Hamburg was being asked to carry 129 pounds again for the Flash Stakes at Saratoga; he made it seem a feather, spurting to the front and leading all the way. Thus for his next start, the Congress Hall Stakes at Saratoga, Hamburg was assigned 134 pounds, an unprecedented burden for a two-year-old, a twelve-pound penalty for excellence; he won by a length from Archduke which carried only 119 pounds.

Two days later, Archduke gained revenge. Carrying 117 pounds, Archduke caught Hamburg, with 129 pounds, right at the end, winning by a head. Madden

97

changed riders for Hamburg, and Hamburg proceeded to win the Rising Generation with 127 pounds, followed by the Electric Handicap with 132 pounds. Thus in his last six races before September, Hamburg as a two-year-old had carried an average of 130 pounds, eight above scale.

By this time, Hamburg had won eight out of ten races and it was conceded no two-year-old could run with him. Madden thereupon entered him in the Flight Stakes against top older horses, something horsemen will not do now. Hamburg went to the front at the start and held the lead to the stretch, where four-year-old Requital, champion as a two-year-old, wore him down and won by two lengths. With but three days rest, Hamburg was sent out again, this time against two-year-olds in the Flatbush Stakes, and led every step but the last, losing by a head to Previous, which had a five-pound weight advantage. Two days later, Hamburg was out again and won the Autumn Stakes with 129 pounds, beating Archduke and others.

Then came the Great Eastern Handicap and Hamburg was assigned a record-high 135 pounds. This was considered an impossible burden and horsemen urged Madden not to accept the assignment; Archduke was weighted closest to him with 124 pounds, and the Futurity winner, L'Alouette, was in with only 120. Hamburg went to the post, however, and stood there with his 135 pounds for a half-hour as Starter C. H. Pettingill had unusual difficulty in lining up the field for an even start. Once away, Hamburg was never headed, winning by a length. Three days later, he won the Prospect with 127 pounds and, two days after that, picked up the Excelsior to conclude his two-year-old campaign with twelve victories in sixteen starts.

On year-end handicaps, champion two-year-olds usually are assigned 126 pounds, their closest rivals a pound or so less, the top fifty colts being ranked within twenty pounds of the champion. From time to time, a really exceptional two-year-old champion will be assigned more than 126 pounds; Secretariat was assigned 129, four more than his closest rival. On the 1897 year-end handicap, Hamburg was paid the compliment of being assigned 140 pounds, ten more than the colt considered second-best of the year, which happened to be Plaudit, also owned by Madden. The only question that remained was whether Hamburg was the greatest two-year-old up to that time. This was answered to some extent when Francis Trevelyan reported in the *New York Journal*, "Even Mr. James R. Keene, who owned Domino, confessed yesterday that Hamburg was a better 2-year-old than Domino."

In later years there were many stories about Hamburg's record-priced sale, none of which Madden bothered to deny. In point of fact, trainer Billy Lakeland arrived at Churchill Downs in Louisville on December 10, 1897, inspected Hamburg, and handed Madden a check signed by bloodstock agent W. L. Powers; Hamburg was insured for $100,000 for his trip back to New York. Besieged by reporters, Madden admitted the price was not as much as $60,000. A week later, Marcus Daly was contacted in Montana and would not deny that he had bought the colt; subsequently, Daly said he had paid "only a little in excess of $40,000, the excess being intended to break the American record."

Madden was quick to reinvest his money. Within a week he paid $5,000 for a weanling colt and a few days later, bought its dam, Peg Woffington. The weanling was named David Garrick, which was unusual. Madden liked to name his horses after people he knew, finding it a useful selling aid, but David Garrick had long since been out of the public eye. He was one of the first great English actors, a contemporary of Peg Woffington, a favorite of Charles II. The name did not lessen the colt's salability, however, for after Madden broke him as a yearling and took him to New York to saddle him for victory in the 1899 Great Trial Stakes, he sold him to Pierre Lorillard for $25,000.

99

Two months after selling Hamburg to Daly, Madden bought 235 acres of Bluegrass land for $30,000. It was located on the Winchester Pike and could be reached from the Phoenix Hotel—where Madden had maintained a suite since he had moved to Lexington seven years earlier—within fifteen minutes behind a good road horse. "I wanted a place near town so, if I had a customer, I could get him out there to see the horse before he changed his mind," Madden said. He named the farm Hamburg Place and within a dozen years, Madden would enlarge it to 2,300 acres and build there the finest, perhaps the most famous, Thoroughbred nursery in Kentucky.

During the early part of the 1898 season, racing men were nodding their heads in agreement that young John E. Madden had put one over on Daly. It appeared that Madden had two nice colts in his barn the previous year, had sold one for a record price, and had kept the better one.

The one he kept was Plaudit, which he had purchased for $6,500 from Ed Brown, a prominent black trainer known as Brown Dick when he was conditioning the Woodburn racers before the Civil War. At two, Plaudit had won minor stakes in Cincinnati for Brown, but when shipped to New York, finished fourth in the Futurity, and Madden bought him. The first time he carried Madden's silks, he upset Dwyer's champion older horse, Ben Brush. Madden wintered him at Churchill Downs, training him to a fine edge for his first start at three. This happened to be the now-famous Kentucky Derby; although a fixture of some local prominence, the Kentucky Derby was of little national consequence in 1898 and only four horses ran for it. Plaudit won it by a neck, then picked up the Clark Stakes; next he won the Oakley Derby at Cincinnati, then was unopposed in the Buckeye Stakes and walked over for his fourth straight victory. Madden shipped him east and immediately sold him to W. C. Whitney for $25,000.

John E. Madden, the compleat horseman

Meanwhile, Hamburg made his first start of the season in the Belmont Stakes and finished third. Billy Lakeland, who had trained Domino, probably did not know how to handle Hamburg's appetite; Hamburg came out at three as a butterball and was far too slow for the Belmont, which Bowling Brook won by six lengths. Lakeland dropped Hamburg back to 1 1/16 miles in the Spring Special and he won galloping. In the seven-furlong Swift Stakes, Hamburg again won easily, by six lengths, pulled up. Questions persisted whether Hamburg could go a distance, leading to a runoff between the two Madden-sold stars, Hamburg and Plaudit, in the 1 5/8-mile Realization. Doubt as to Hamburg's staying ability was quickly dispelled: He took the lead in the Realization at the start and led all the way, Plaudit never threatening him. Three weeks later, Hamburg made his final start, winning the 2 1/4-mile Brighton Cup by a margin arbitrarily estimated at one-sixteenth of a mile.

Hamburg then was retired to Daly's Bitter Root Stud in Montana. He stood only two seasons there because Daly died in 1900; at the Bitter Root dispersal, Madden bought Hamburg for $60,000 acting as agent for W. C. Whitney. Hamburg then stood at Whitney's La Belle Stud in Kentucky until Whitney's death in 1904. The owner's son, H. P. Whitney, bought Hamburg for $70,000 and stood him at Brookdale Stud in New Jersey. America's leading sire in 1905, Hamburg sent out such champions as Artful, Hamburg Belle, Dandelion, Burgomaster, and Borrow.

In 1898 W. C. Whitney decided to retire from politics (former secretary of the navy) and active participation in business (New York City transit companies, utilities, tobacco trusts, and sundry other endeavors which netted him several million dollars a year) and devote his time to the sport of racing. His was a simple approach. He asked John Madden to serve as his consultant, and he proceeded to buy up every good horse in sight. Madden bought Jean Bereaud, best two-year-old of the year, for $30,000 on Whitney's account. He sold Whitney champion Admiration for $15,000, DeLacy for $12,000, Suburban winner Tillo for $10,000, champion Kilmarnack for $20,000. In 1901 Madden sold Whitney four champions, Yankee, Endurance by Right, Blue Girl, Gunfire, and acted as agent in the purchase of champion Nasturtium, for a total of $150,000. "There's no trick to selling horses," Madden said later, "so long as you're selling good horses." As might be expected, Whitney quickly became America's leading owner.

Madden secured for Whitney one of the great horse trainers of all time, Sam Hildreth, who had scored some success in the Midwest at the time and much later was to reign for nine years as America's leading trainer. In New York for the first time, Hildreth, who was part Indian, did well with the Whitney champions, but in 1900, a Kingston colt named Ballyhoo Bey (which Madden had sold Whitney as a yearling for $12,000) lost his first start. This should not have happened, Whitney was advised. Shortly thereafter, Whitney and Hildreth parted company and Madden supervised the training of the Whitney horses until another trainer could be found. Initially, Hildreth was not distressed over leaving Whitney. The *New York Times* reported in October of that year that Hildreth had won some $250,000 in bets, stakes, and purses since leaving Whitney and had a stable of thirty horses valued at $100,000.

On the evening of October 1, 1900, Hildreth had too much to drink. Upon some provocation not reported, he assaulted a waiter in the Morris Park dining room and then wandered off into the infield firing a pistol. He was headed for serious trouble. The following day the *Morning Telegraph* reported:

John E. Madden, a horse owner and trainer of W. C. Whitney's horses, was assaulted and knocked down near the Morris Park race course last night by Samuel J. Hildreth, who was succeeded by Madden in Mr. Whitney's employ. Mr. Hildreth's friends say that overindulgence in liquor was at the bottom of the trouble, but it is asserted by Mr. Madden's acquaintances that there was ill feeling on Hildreth's part due to his having been supplanted by his opponent. The assault occurred in the little restaurant near the race track.

Green B. Morris, W. P. Burch, and several other racing men were in the dining room at 7 o'clock last evening when Hildreth suddenly entered. He had been celebrating his recent great Turf successes and appeared somewhat flushed. Striding forward, he jerked a thick oaken walking stick from one of the men present, and advancing down the dining room, began pulling cups, saucers, and plates off the tables with the crook of the stick. Madden saw him approaching and called out, "Good evening, Mr. Hildreth."

Without a word in reply, Hildreth seized the heavy stick in both hands and brought it down upon Madden's head over the right eye with such force that the stick broke into two. The blow felled Madden to the floor, but he sprang up again.

Madden now knocked Hildreth down and, falling upon him, caught him by the throat and held him fast. Thinking there might be pistol play between the combatants, the spectators now scrambled out of the room in great excitement.

Holding him with a fierce grip, Madden then looked Hildreth in the eye and exclaimed: "Are you sorry for what you have done? If you are, apologize and I will let you up."

The apology was issued immediately. Hildreth was an intelligent man and it was obvious that anyone who could absorb that kind of opening blow was not one with whom a man need hesitate with trivial formalities.

Something further should be noted about Madden's handling of Ballyhoo Bey. Turf historians, either through kindness or want of evidence, failed to record the number of trainers who improved on a horse taken from Hildreth's care. Madden saddled Ballyhoo Bey only twice. He won both times. The first time was the Futurity, the richest and most important race of the year. The race figured to be taken by James R. Keene, Whitney's bitter rival on Wall Street, who had entered three really good horses: Cap and Bells, which had won two stakes and the next season was to become the first American filly to win the English

104

Oaks; Tommy Atkins, also winner of two stakes; and Olympian which had placed in several stakes.

Whitney called home from England the most famous rider of the day, Tod Sloan, to ride Ballyhoo Bey. Years later, Winnie O'Connor, who rode Tommy Atkins, revealed, "We talked it over among ourselves and decided that if we could run Sloan and Ballyhoo Bey into a pocket, they'd never get out, and one of the three of us would come on to win. We knew that our mounts had the race to themselves."

For the first part of the race, things went pretty much as the three Keene jockeys had planned. Harry Spencer had Cap and Bells on the lead, Milton Henry kept Olympian lapped on her, and O'Connor on Tommy Atkins had Ballyhoo Bey walled up on the rail. Coming into the stretch, however, Cap and Bells began to tire. O'Connor yelled to Henry to drop over on the rail in the filly's place to keep in Ballyhoo Bey's path, while he on Tommy Atkins could draw off on the outside and win. But such is avarice among thieves. With nothing in front of him, Henry figured he was in the best position to know who was going to win this race—and the devil take the hindmost. He put Olympian into a drive. That did it. The trap was opened. Sloan slipped Ballyhoo Bey through on the rail and won by 1 1/2 lengths, Olympian second, Tommy Atkins third. It was, Whitney declared, "my most satisfying Turf success."

In truth, the Keene horses probably were better than Ballyhoo Bey; he carried seventeen pounds less than did Tommy Atkins. A week later, however, Madden sent Ballyhoo Bey out again for the Flatbush Stakes and he gave Tommy Atkins five pounds and a beating.

Thereafter, Madden turned over the Whitney horses to John W. Rogers to train. Madden had his own sizable stable to race and sell. The following year, 1901, Madden ranked second (to Whitney) on the owners' list and ranked first on the trainers' list; the horses he had saddled earned $127,090. The next year, he again was the nation's

105

leading trainer, setting an earnings record of $150,476. In 1903 horses he trained earned $118,304, and the *Thoroughbred Record* noted: "Mr. Madden is the only millionaire breeder of Thoroughbreds who trains, develops and races his own horses. He leaves nothing to chance. Every detail about his stable—the quantity and quality of feed, ventilation, disposition of every horse, the kindness of attendants—is planned by Mr. Madden and must be rigorously carried out. The secret of Mr. Madden's success is a bright mind, a sound body, unbounded energy, and an efficiency that approaches genius, so perfectly has he applied it to every department of the breeding and racing industry."

Madden made his first million buying untried horses cheaply, training them, developing the potential he had seen—that others had not—into top racehorses which he sold well. For example, in 1906 Madden saw something in a two-year-old gelding which had finished second in his first start and purchased him for $3,700. This was Salvidere; within two months, Madden had saddled Salvidere for six consecutive stakes victories and purses amounting to $53,420. Congratulated for developing the gelding into the leading two-year-old of the season, Madden disclaimed responsibility: "Horses make men. Men don't make horses. Many a turfman's reputation is made by a horse that he least expected would turn out to be great. A man may be fortunate to discover something in the horse that the previous owner had overlooked. On this discovery, the future success of a horse frequently hinges. That is all luck."

Such luck hounded Madden. His singular talent in training, developing horses, eventually made breeders and other trainers wary of selling him a prospect cheaply. When Madden's gaze was arrested by a horse, its selling price immediately rose.

Thomas Murphy of Louisville claimed he once beat Madden $50 on a trade. Madden had visited his farm, looked at his yearlings, picked out one, and offered $3,000.

"Surely you're not talking about my $10,000 colt!" Murphy exclaimed. There ensued some discussion of the colt's obvious conformation defects, his unfashionable pedigree, the uncommon poor market for racehorses, and other topics calculated to reach some negotiable price range, but Murphy stood firm at $4,500. Madden could see no more than $4,250 in the colt; he returned to his hotel.

"Well, I got to thinking," Murphy said. "There it was, snowing, in the dead of winter, and a horse is worth no more than what you can get for it, so with my mind made up, I drove to town." Murphy found Madden having dinner, went to his table, and asked, "Say, were you trying to call me? Several people told me you were looking for me so I thought I better come in and see what you wanted." Madden didn't fall for that one.

" 'No, I didn't call you,' Madden said. 'You came in here to sell me that horse, didn't you?' Well, he had me there so I told him he could have the horse for $4,300, and I would give him $100 to take the colt off my place.

" 'Give me the hundred,' Madden said. I did and then he asked, 'Were you going to sell me that horse for $4,250?' I admitted I was and he kinda smiled. 'Not a bad trade. I mailed you a check for $4,500 just before dinner, so you made $150 and I made $100.' "

Not so much because he was tired of haggling over horse trades—for Madden continued to enjoy trading horses almost until he died—but because he believed he could breed and raise good horses cheaper than he could buy them, Madden bought Hamburg Place. There he was to assemble the largest band of Thoroughbred broodmares in America. Initially, Madden took the Hamburg Place foals to the track and sold them after they had established their racing form. In the spring of 1908 he shipped fifty-four two-year-olds and several other older horses for which he had not yet received his price to the Bennings track in Washington, D.C. By season's end he had sold all the horses in his barn and in the process had earned $171,317 in purses to rank second on the owners' list, and had saddled horses for himself and others that earned $249,106 to rank second on the trainers' list. Among the Hamburg Place two-year-olds he had that year were Sir Martin, recognized as champion of the division, and Fayette, thought by many to be better than Sir Martin—which is traditional to the Turf, the observer's unshakable confidence in his superior knowledge of another man's horse.

What Sir Martin and Fayette did not win in the way of New York stakes for two-year-olds was picked up by two other Madden colts, Edward and Joe Madden, and three stakes-winning fillies, Lady Bedford, Lawton Wiggins, and Miss Kearney. On December 8, 1908, Madden sold Sir Martin to Louis Winans for $75,000; shipped to England, Sir Martin was the first American-bred to start as betting favorite for the Epsom Derby, but fell at the final turn. Madden bought him back as a stallion for Hamburg Place, where he died in 1930.

Winans's English trainer was Vivian Gooch. Seven years later, Gooch visited Hamburg Place, and over dinner, Madden made him a gift of the foal Sir Martin's dam was carrying. The following spring, Lady Sterling produced a chestnut colt by Star Shoot, which Madden registered as being bred in partnership with Gooch. When the colt was weaned, Madden bought back Gooch's interest and sent the colt to the races. He started him four times as a two-year-old, got no part of a purse, and then sold him for $10,000 to Commander J. K. L. Ross of Canada. The colt was Sir Barton, which did not win a race until he was three. The first race he won was the Kentucky Derby; three days later, he took the Preakness, then the Withers, and later added the Belmont Stakes, to become America's first Triple Crown winner. He came from Hamburg Place.

Thoroughbred racing was in serious trouble in New York in 1908. Governor Charles Evans Hughes, who a few years later went to sleep confident he had defeated Woodrow Wilson for the presidency of the United States, was forever saying he did not mind horse racing so much, but he was opposed to betting. Resultant antibetting legislation soon reduced purses and track attendance and finally stopped all horse racing in New York after 1910. (This just goes to show how times change; today, New York politicians do not care about horse racing, but they want *more* betting, which conceivably could cause racing to stop again in New York as it was in 1911–1912.)

As purses dropped, then disappeared in New York, the market for racehorses fell the same way. While racing was to continue in Kentucky and Maryland, with minor meetings in Utah and Montana, the horse industry more or less collapsed under the weight of antiracing legislation in nearly all the states where racing once flourished. James Ben Ali Haggin, who for the previous twenty years had been America's largest breeder of Thoroughbreds, dispersed his studs and racing stables, selling horses by the carload, wherever he could find a market—in the United States, Europe, and South America. Kentucky's most prominent commercial breeders, Colonel Milton Young of McGrathiana Stud and Colonel E. F. Clay and Colonel Catesby Woodford of Runnymede Stud, also dispersed their studs. Mares worth $20,000 before racing was outlawed in New York brought $300.

Madden always believed a good time to buy a horse was when another man wanted to sell. When the market collapsed, Madden sold nothing; he bought. In 1912 he bought all thirty-five of Colonel Clay's mares, plus yearlings and sucklings—and Star Shoot. At Runnymede, Star Shoot had been America's leading sire in 1911–1912. At Hamburg Place, Star Shoot was to lead the sire lists three more times, in 1916, 1917, and 1919. Star Shoot sired two of the best horses Madden ever bred—Triple Crown winner Sir Barton, and Grey Lag, champion at three, four, and five. Madden sold Grey Lag as a yearling for $10,000 to Max Hirsch, one of America's great trainers, who won the rich Champagne Stakes with Grey Lag as a two-year-old.

Sam Hildreth was putting together a stable for Harry Sinclair, much as Madden had for W. C. Whitney twenty years earlier. Hildreth asked Hirsch for a price on Grey Lag and got one promptly, $40,000. "I could have said $15,000 or $20,000 just as easily," Hirsch said later, "but $40,000 just happened to come to mind and Hildreth didn't blink, just said he would have to see the colt first." Inspection revealed an odd patch of gray hair, normally obscured by a saddle cloth; Hildreth was superstitious and declared he would not have the oddly marked horse at any price. A few days later, however, Sinclair saw Hirsch and asked him about his Champagne winner. Hirsch told him that his trainer already had seen Grey Lag and had turned him down.

"Never mind that," said the man who about then also was negotiating for the oil rights on government property that would gusher into the Teapot Dome scandal, "just name a price." Hirsch casually added $20,000 for the gray patch, and Sinclair said, "Fine, he's my horse." For $60,000, Sinclair purchased one of the great racehorses of the 1920s, winner of $136,715.

When racing was revived in New York in 1913, Madden never resumed an active role as a trainer. Much of his time was devoted to Hamburg Place and its extensive breeding operation. He purchased more land. In 1917 he bought 830 acres of Elmendorf Farm from the Haggin estate with the first million dollar check ever to clear a Lexington bank. Five years later, he resold the land at a handsome profit to Joseph and George Widener. Records on breeders were not maintained until 1917. With more mares than any other breeder, Madden probably was America's leading breeder long before 1916, but of record, he led America's breeders in races won for the first eleven years such records were kept, from 1917 through

1927, and in purses earned for eight of the first nine years. In 1921 horses bred at Hamburg Place won 424 races, and in 1923 they won 419 races; no other breeder since then has bred horses which have won as many as 400 races in a single year.

These records are largely the result of quantity. As to quality, Madden bred 182 stakes winners; he was the first man to breed as many as five Kentucky Derby winners—Old Rosebud (1914), Sir Barton (1919), Paul Jones (1920), Zev (1923), and Flying Ebony (1925); he also bred five winners of the Belmont Stakes—Joe Madden (1909), The Finn (1915), Sir Barton (1919), Grey Lag (1921), and Zev (1923). When Madden died in 1929, he had credit for breeding America's only Triple Crown winner in Sir Barton, America's leading money winner in Zev ($313,639), and America's leading money-earning filly in Princess Doreen ($174,745). In his time, John E. Madden was the most successful and—with the possible exception of David Harum—the most well-known seller of horses in America. In his later years, as he gradually retired from the horse business, he increased his fortune considerably with investments in securities.

"In my youth, it was a word and blow, and I could knock down most of those with whom I argued," he was to say. "After a while, it dawned on me that while I could knock a man down, I never could make him like it. So I changed my tactics, and instead of knocking them down, I began slapping them on the back. And you know, I began making money from that hour."

MAN O' WAR

O<small>F ALL THE</small> great horses which have thundered over the American Turf, one towers above them all. "If I wanted him to walk, he wanted to jog," said his trainer, Louis C. Feustel. "If I wanted him to jog, he wanted to gallop. No matter what I wanted, he wanted to go faster."

That was Man o' War. His very name suggests strength, power. He was a superhorse, of greater dimensions than previous champions. He was taller than most horses, growing to 16.2 hands. He held his head higher than most horses, and this, together with an impatience with restraint, lent pomp and circumstance to his way of going, an air of majesty. He did not beat his rivals, he conquered them.

Foaled in 1917 at August Belmont, Jr.'s Nursery Stud five miles north of Lexington on the Georgetown Pike, Man o' War was born in an era of sports superheroes. After General Black Jack Pershing had led the American Expeditionary Forces to end the war that was to end all wars, a brash, young, affluent America entered upon an age of frivolity. Effect of the newly enacted federal income tax was unknown, paper wealth was found by everyone in the stock market and flaunted, constitutional prohibition of alcohol was flouted. Old moral standards were set aside, and the calm measured step of the Mauve Decade before World War I quickened to the two-step and then the Charleston as America danced to a sound out of Chicago called New Orleans jazz. It was a time when an extraordinary crop of creative writers dramatized sports for a receptive audience that was yet to be distracted by movies and television; developing a new jargon to describe sports figures, Grantland Rice, Ring Lardner, Heywood Broun, Stanley Woodard magnified stars into superstars whose feats have since been surpassed, but even now cannot be forgotten.

When Man 0' War was two, Jack Dempsey won the heavyweight title and seventeen-year-old Bobby Jones wore knickers in the national golf finals. When Man o' War was three and smashed all records for purses own, and time for the mile, 1 1/8 miles, 1 3/8 miles, 1 1/2 miles, and 1 5/8 miles, Babe Ruth hit fifty-four home runs for the first time, George Gipp was an All American at Notre Dame, and Big Bill Tilden introduced the big serve to Wimbledon, Titans they were, giants of the game.

Horses have run faster and horses have earned more money than Man o' War, but the fame of Big Red lingers. This is due in no small measure to the coming in 1931 to Faraway Farm near Lexington, where Man o' War stood as America's premier sire, of an epic poet; this was groom Will Harbut who took charge of Big Red and his legend. The thousands who trekked to Faraway to see America's greatest Thoroughbred were enthralled: ". . . and he look over to that Whitney hoss and he say, 'Now you come on, Grier, iffin you can' . . . and a man comes here and offers a million dollars for him and Mr. Riddles says, 'No, lots of men might have a million dollahs, but only one man can have Man o' War . . . stand still, Red . . . 'cause, he wuz de mostest hoss. . . .''

Man o' War was the apex of accomplishment in some thirty-five years of breeding Thoroughbreds for August Belmont, Jr., and he happened to come along during the nadir of Belmont's business career. Born in 1853 and educated at Harvard, the younger Belmont joined his

113

father's banking house and became a full partner in 1885.

August Belmont, Sr., had come to America in 1845 as a representative of the Rothschilds and built a financial fortress on Wall Street. "Had he been as bold in business as he was outside it," noted the *New York World*, "he might have been the richest banker in America. His mastery of finance was perfect. But he chose the safer course—the course which had been steered for years by the houses of foreign birth and parentage—and was content with a fortune estimated anywhere from five to ten million dollars. Up to within a couple of years ago the house dealt almost exclusively in foreign exchange, which is by no means the most profitable known to bankers. On March 15, 1888, the house was reorganized and new blood was infused into it; since then, it is said, it has made much greater profits than ever."

The new blood here was August Belmont, Jr., who headed the company after his father's death in 1890. Unlike his conservative father, the younger Belmont tried new fields of investment. He was the first banker to show interest in a subway system in New York City. This was to bring him in combat with William Collins Whitney and Thomas Fortune Ryan who controlled surface public transportation in New York.

Whitney, who was to found a Turf dynasty carried on by his sons and today by his grandchildren John Hay Whitney and C. V. Whitney, after a term as secretary of the navy, formed the Metropolitan Street Railway Company which bought up most of the horse-drawn car lines, replaced them with cable cars, and then converted these to streetcars powered by electricity.

In 1890 young Belmont had been appointed to the Rapid Transit Commission for New York, and his conviction that subways would provide the best public transportation was persistently opposed by Whitney. By 1900, however, the Rapid Transit Commission asked for bids on construction of a subway on the West Side of Man-

114

hattan. Construction costs of the subway were to be borne by the city. John B. McDonald was awarded the job on a low bid of $35 million, but was unable to post the $1 million bond (the bonding company's unexpected refusal being attributed, correctly or not, to Whitney and Ryan). Belmont then stepped in, posting bond and triumphing over some delaying tactics by Whitney, obtained a state charter for a new company, the Interborough Rapid Transit Company, and work began on the West Side subway. Soon thereafter, demand arose for an East Side subway, and Whitney's Metropolitan petitioned the commission for permission to build it, a move which by 1906 brought about the merger of the Belmont and Whitney transit companies into one Interborough-Metropolitan Company. Belmont, said to have made $6 million on construction of the subway, another million on sale to Interborough of a mule tram line in the Bronx, was subject of a stockholder's suit charging Belmont's profits unconscionable. The suit was dismissed, Cornelius Vanderbilt testifying that Belmont's compensation was not abnormal, but "modest." There were those who complained that Vanderbilt was a poor judge of what comprised modest compensation, but the judge ruled that "Mr. Belmont's stock was a usual payment to a man who put an enterprise on its feet."

In 1909 Belmont conceived the idea of building an eight-mile canal across Cape Cod that would shorten by seventy-five miles shipping routes from Boston to New York and avoid dangerous waters. The idea was based on a sorely inaccurate engineering estimate that construction would cost $5 million and take two years. In truth, it was to cost $16 million and take five years. Belmont buried his fortune in the Cape Cod canal, borrowing heavily. As months and years of construction dragged by, enthusiasm of other investors waned, and Belmont became more deeply involved. When finally completed, the canal never did prove to be a money maker. The canal's biggest year was 1924, when gross income from tolls exceeded operating expenses by some $272,000. After Belmont's death, his executors were able to recoup some of the Belmont losses by selling the canal to the government for $11.5 million. During Belmont's life, however, the financial drain caused by the canal was one of the reasons Belmont decided to sell his yearling crop of 1918, divesting himself of his greatest achievement in racing, Man o' War.

Belmont's achievements in racing were many. His father had been a leader of the movement which revitalized racing in New York after the Civil War. President of the American Jockey Club, which built and operated Jerome Park near Fordham, and one of six founders of elegant old Monmouth Park in New Jersey, the elder Belmont bought Glenelg as a $2,000 yearling and in him found the best three-year-old of 1869, winner of the Travers and Jerome and second to his stablemate Fenian in the classic race named for his owner. The trophy won by Fenian in the 1869 Belmont Stakes was returned more than a half-century later to the race course built by the son and named for the father, and today remains a challenge trophy, retained for one year by the owner of the winner of the Belmont Stakes at Belmont Park. The elder Belmont had established 1,000-acre Nursery Stud at Babylon on Long Island in 1867, but by 1885 had decided that there must be something in the climate or soil of Kentucky that was better suited for raising racehorses and transferred his Thoroughbred breeding operation to a farm he leased near Lexington.

During his father's lifetime, the younger Belmont viewed as a spectator his father's racing and breeding success with such champions as Glenelg, Woodbine, Olitipa, Sultana, Susquehanna, Raceland, Potomac, La Tosca, and Fides. Upon his father's death, the younger Belmont decided to enter racing, and his success in and influence on the sport far surpassed that of his father.

In 1891, when the younger Belmont took up the lease on Nursery Stud near Lexington and began assembling a racing and breeding operation around a nucleus of stock purchased from his father's dispersal, there was dire need for rehabilitation of the sport in New York. The socially prominent men in his father's generation who had revived the sport in 1866 had passed from the scene and racing had slipped into disrepute, counted a public nuisance. Legislation in New York, New Jersey, and other states had been passed outlawing gambling and, indirectly, horse racing.

Belmont was among the leaders who resisted the closing of race courses. Test cases were brought; the devious ploy of betting with a bookmaker, orally, with no posting of odds on a slate and no written record of the wager maintained by the bookmaker, was duly tried in court and was won by racing enthusiasts.

In 1894 The Jockey Club was organized with fifty founding members; racing rules were promulgated, and nonconflicting racing dates were allocated to Metropolitan tracks; licenses issued by The Jockey Club were required for participants in racing; The Jockey Club purchased Colonel Sanders Bruce's *American Stud Book* and thus became the official registrar for Thoroughbreds. In 1895 the New York legislature created a state racing commission to regulate and supervise horse racing in the state; August Belmont, Jr., was appointed its chairman. The racing commission reinforced with governmental authority the control of the sport by The Jockey Club by adopting the rules of The Jockey Club, approving its appointment of racing officials, and prohibiting participation in the sport without licensing by The Jockey Club. Succeeding to the chairmanship of the club in 1895 was August Belmont, Jr.

Conflict of interest did not seem to trouble Belmont. He simultaneously served as commission chairman and operator of the transit companies the commission supervised, and as commission chairman and Jockey Club steward while operating race tracks and owning horses racing under the supervision of the commission and The

Jockey Club. A man wishing to breed to America's leading stallion, to apply for a foal registration, to request stalls at Belmont Park, to complain of a foul in a race by a Belmont horse, or to renew his owner's license—today he would be heard by five different individuals, private boards, or governmental bodies—at the turn of the century, need have seen only one man, August Belmont, Jr.

In 1900 when they merged their transit interests, Belmont and Whitney joined in the purchase and rebuilding of Saratoga Race Course. Shortly thereafter, they joined in the purchase of property on Long Island where they built Belmont Park, of which Belmont became president. These two courses remain today the sites of America's most important races.

In the 1890s Belmont purchased and raced champions Lady Violet, Henry of Navarre, and Belmont winner Hastings. The first great horse he bred was Beldame; she won a pair of minor stakes as a two-year-old in 1903, but her promise aroused dispute between her owner and her trainer, J. J. Hyland. In October of that year, Belmont had other things on his mind. These included the building of New York's subways, financing Judge Alton Parker's unsuccessful presidential bid against rough-riding, antitrust man Teddy Roosevelt, and building Belmont Park. He felt he had more to do than argue with his trainer over a two-year-old filly that could not beat W. C. Whitney's Armenia or Hamburg Belle, owned by Whitney's son-in-law, so he leased Beldame to Newton Bennington.

Beldame thereupon demonstrated she was one of the four or five greatest three-year-old fillies in the history of the Turf, carrying Bennington's colors to victory in twelve of fourteen races, beating fillies pointless, handling colts with ease, giving weight to the best older horses and whipping them without effort, at distances from six furlongs to 1 3/4 miles. The next season Belmont took her back, and although she won only two of ten races as a four-year-old, one of these was the historic Suburban Handicap, which only one other filly had won previously.

Beldame was retired from racing as only the third filly, after Miss Woodford and Firenze, to earn more than $100,000.

Among the 129 stakes winners Belmont bred at Nursery Stud, Beldame was the best filly and Fair Play was the best colt to carry his colors in America. Fair Play was by Hastings, which twice led America's sire lists, but he had the misfortune to be foaled in 1905. That year, about five miles east of Nursery Stud at James R. Keene's Castleton Stud were foaled two better runners—Colin, which Fair Play could not beat in five tries (but then, no other horse ever beat Colin, either), and Celt, counted by such an astute Turf observer as Walter Vosburgh as being as good as Colin.

At three, Fair Play finished first or second in fifteen of his sixteen races, and after both Colin and Celt were retired in June, had things much his own way in the richest races for three-year-olds, winding up as leading money earner of the division. He ran in track-record times at 1 1/4 miles, 1 5/16 miles, 1 1/2 miles, won at 1 5/8 miles and 1 3/4 miles. He could stay. As a stallion he topped the sire list in 1920, 1924, and 1927 and long has been considered American breeding's most important native source of stamina. He sired an extraordinary number of top horses, forty-seven stakes winners, and was the first stallion in the world to sire as many as six $100,000 earners: Display, Mad Hatter, Chance Shot, Chance Play, Mad Play, and Man o' War.

Man o' War was foaled on March 29, 1917, at Nursery Stud and was recognized as something apart from the start, for he had uncommonly long legs, a fiery red coat, and a presumption the world was his.

His breeder regarded the colt, named as a yearling by Mrs. Belmont, as the best of the crop, and he briefly considered retaining him when in 1918 he decided to sell most of his yearling crop. With the Quartermaster Corps in Spain procuring supplies for the American Expeditionary Forces, Major Belmont figured he would be re-moved from the racing scene for some time and could use the money; three weeks before the Saratoga auction, he instructed his farm manager to include Man o' War among the twenty-one yearlings offered for sale. The group was offered privately, at prices ranging from $30,000 to $42,000, but there were no takers. At auction the yearlings brought $51,450, so several people were sorely wrong here.

One who was not wrong was Louis C. Feustel. As a boy he had taken his first job exercising horses at Belmont's Long Island farm where he exercised Hastings. Later as stable foreman, he was closely associated with Fair Play. Later still, as a trainer of a division of the Belmont stable, he had saddled Mahubah, Man o' War's dam, for her only victory. He knew the pedigree, and he had inspected the colt at Nursery Stud before he was shipped to Saratoga. Long after Man o' War had left his greatness of the race track for greatness of legend, Feustel recalled with de-tachment his first sight of the colt: "Very tall and gan-gling, he was thin and so on the leg as to give the same ungainly impression one gets in seeing a week-old foal." He liked him, although he confessed he thought some of the other Belmont yearlings might be better.

As trainer for Samuel D. Riddle, Feustel got Man o' War for $5,000 at Saratoga. In view of Man o' War's sub-sequent success, and yearling prices of today, $5,000 has been reported to be an absurdly low price. However, the average price for all yearlings sold at Saratoga that year was only $1,038, and Man o' War was the sixth-highest-priced yearling of the auction. Highest price of the sale was $15,600, paid for Golden Broom by Mrs. Riddle's niece Mrs. Walter M. Jeffords, Sr.

Feustel set about breaking Man o' War at Saratoga shortly after the sale. He gave a leg up to Harry Vititoe, a good exercise boy, who promptly was discarded by the yearling; Man o' War roamed about the grounds for some

The majesty of Man o' War at three, Clarence Kummer up

Samuel D. Riddle,
owner of Man o' War

August Belmont,
breeder of Man o' War

(New York Racing Association)

time before he was caught. Thereafter he gave little trouble, for, although he was high spirited, he was not quarrelsome. In the fall Man o' War was shipped to training quarters in Berlin, Maryland, along with Golden Broom, and in a final speed trial of a quarter-mile, Golden Broom beat Man o' War by a half-length. This prompted a thought, which lasted about six months, that Golden Broom was in the same class with Man o' War.

Man o' War was shipped to old Havre de Grace in the spring of 1919, caught cold and ran a temperature of 106. The fire of the Fair Plays outburned the fever, however, and he was back to work within a week. Feustel brought him along slowly, schooling him at the barrier at Pimlico and then shipping to New York.

Man o' War did not slip up on anybody. He was 3-5 for his first start on June 6 down the old Widener Chute at Belmont Park, and Johnny Loftus brought him back by six lengths in fifty-nine seconds as a field of maidens went five furlongs.

Three days later he was back for the 5 1/2-furlong Keene Memorial Stakes against a good colt, On Watch, sired by Fair Play's nemesis, Colin. Man o' War did not get the lead until the stretch, but won easily by three lengths in 1:05 3/5.

Loftus had been working Man o' War in the morning, schooling him to get away from the barrier faster. For the Youthful he worked the colt five furlongs in track-record time, and on June 21 he broke first and led throughout the 5 1/2-furlong Youthful, giving On Watch twelve pounds and a 2 1/2-length beating. Both the Keene Memorial and Youthful were on off tracks, which never made much difference to Man o' War.

Two days later he was brought out for the five-furlong Hudson Stakes and was asked to carry 130 pounds. A two-year-old in June carrying 130 pounds would seem an outrageous thing today, but bettors then thought nothing of it and clamored for Man o' War at 1-10. He won, eased up, giving his closet rival, Violet Tip, twenty-one pounds.

A touch of colic kept Man o' War out of the Great American Stakes, but he was back within a week and picked up the six-furlong Tremont Stakes easily enough with 130 pounds, giving Ralco fifteen pounds and a one-length beating.

Shipped to Saratoga and given a month's rest after the Tremont, Man o' War was brought out for the United States Hotel Stakes and was carrying his usual burden of 130 pounds, giving fifteen pounds to H. P. Whitney's Upset. He dispatched this rival with ease, winning by two lengths.

About this time, Mrs. Jeffords's trainer, Mike Daly, suggested to Feustel that inasmuch as Golden Broom and Man o' War appeared to be the best of the crop, they might just as well alternate stakes. Daly's tone perhaps suggested that he was doing Feustel and Man o' War a favor. Out of this came a private match at three furlongs. Loftus was not available and Carroll Shilling rode Man o' War. A few jumps from the start it became known that Man o' War had the thing and he went along in even eighths of :11, :11, and :11, beating Golden Broom by a length. It was this performance, Feustel later recalled, that convinced Riddle he had a champion.

In August at Saratoga, by tradition, horsemen seem to recognize certain two-year-olds as sensational. Man o' War was one of these. Sir Barton had won the Kentucky Derby, Preakness, and Belmont, but no one at the time had thought of imitating the British by calling these three races the Triple Crown, and as a consequence Sir Barton was just another nice three-year-old. On the other hand, the younger Man o' War whose overpowering speed had brought him down six times in as many starts, was the talk of the Turf. Just for that he was beaten.

Much has been written of Man o' War's only defeat, little of it reported the same way. Usually, blame is laid on

Loftus, who is said to have had Man o' War facing the wrong way at the start; frequently blame is placed on old C. H. Pettingill, who was substituting for Mars Cassidy as starter.

For the six-furlong Sanford Memorial at Saratoga on August 13, Man o' War was 1-2 with 130 pounds. Golden Broom also carried 130 and was 5-2. Upset carried 115 and was 8-1. G. W. Loft's Donnacona had 112 and was 30-1, T. F. Henry's The Swimmer had 115 and was 50-1, W. R. Coe's Armistice had 112 and was 50-1, and John Madden's Capt. Alcock had 112 and was 100-1.

The start was poor—"straggling," trainer Feustel later recalled—but two horses, The Swimmer and Capt. Alcock, came away slower than Man o' War. Golden Broom, fresh from winning the Saratoga Special, was quickest away, followed closely by Upset and Donnacona. Looking for a way to make up ground, Loftus aimed Man o' War for the rail on the turn. He saved ground, but when Golden Broom began to tire in front, Willie Knapp elected to station Upset a head on the lead just outside, while Donnacona was lapped on Man o' War. There he was, all dressed up with no place to go. At the eighth pole, Loftus finally decided he never would get through on the inside, so he swung off the rail and began to drive. It was too late. Upset, getting fifteen pounds, hung on to win by a half-length.

A contemporary writer observed: "Man o' War is the champion. He never was so great as he was in defeat. . . . He overcame two of his rider's errors and would have made amends for the third if it had not been committed so close to the winning post. He stood a drive such as no other colt has been asked to do in the last 20 years without flinching. . . . Never will his courage be questioned henceforth. It was an unknown quality, for he had never before been put to test. When the test came, he was not found wanting."

Upset was a nice colt, winner of the Latonia Derby the next year, but Man o' War beat him the six other times the two met. Ten days after the Sanford, the two met again in the Grand Union Hotel Stakes; Man o' War carried 130 pounds again, giving Upset five, and was 1-2. He led throughout, winning eased up, beating Upset by a length, with Blazes third.

Man o' War held up the start of the Hopeful Stakes for some twelve minutes ("He was in position No. 3, when he was in any"), and then ran off to win by four lengths from W. R. Coe's grand filly, Cleopatra, with Upset finishing fifth.

He had carried 130 pounds in six consecutive races and for the Futurity he got in light, 127 pounds, ten more than H. P. Whitney's John P. Grier (making his first stakes start), five more than Sam Hildreth's Dominique, the second favorite, seven more than Upset, and ten more than Cleopatra, which had just beaten Upset in the Champagne.

Dominique and John P. Grier set the pace for the first half-mile, then Man o' War came along, passed them easily, and won by 2 1/2 lengths over John P. Grier, with Dominique another four lengths back, trailed by such good horses as Cleopatra, Upset, Paul Jones, On Watch, Dr. Clark, Capt. Alcock, and Miss Jemima.

C. C. Ridley of the *Daily Racing Form* in handicapping the coming three-year-olds of 1920 listed Man o' War at 136 pounds, Blazes next at 120, Upset at 116. Man o' War was unwound at Belmont Park and sent to Berlin, Maryland, for the winter. He grew like a weed. At Saratoga he had weighed 970 pounds, and at Belmont in the fall he had weighed 1,020. That winter he was to grow to 1,150 pounds and 16.2 hands with a girth of 72 inches. He looked the part he was to play.

Man o' War was not entered in the Kentucky Derby. Riddle contended that the race came too early to ask a three-year-old to carry scale weight over 1 1/4 miles. So the Kentucky Derby was left for Paul Jones to beat Upset by a head while Man o' War trained for the 1 1/8-mile Preakness eight days later. Feustel thought his charge was a trifle fine for his first start, but Man o' War rushed off to a four-length lead and coasted home by 1 1/2 lengths over the Whitney pair of Upset and Wildair.

Feustel said his horse improved in the next eleven days. That he did. Under restraint all the way, Man o' War won the Withers Mile by two lengths over Wildair, crossing the finish "under a stout pull" by Clarence Kummer (Johnny Loftus was ruled off the Turf in 1920). Time for the mile was 1:35 4/5, two-fifths of a second faster than Fairy Wand's American record.

By the time the Belmont Stakes came around on June 12, nobody was interested in challenging him any more; only Donnacona was sent for second money. "Under a hard pull," Man o' War won off by twenty lengths. Time for the 1 3/8 miles was 2:14 1/5, another American record, bettering by 3 2/5 seconds the mark Sir Barton had set a year earlier. Although this distance has been run faster on grass, Man o' War's record for 1 3/8 miles on dirt still stands.

Ten days after the Belmont, Man o' War was given to the handicapper in the mile Stuyvesant Handicap and came back with 135 pounds, thirty-two more than his only rival, Yellow Hand; nonetheless, he won by eight lengths in a canter.

It then became extremely difficult to get anyone to run against him, owners being reluctant to have their horses humiliated. Trainer James Rowe, Sr., probably was the only man in America still unconvinced. He had sent H. P. Whitney's horses against Man o' War seven times, beating him once with Upset, finishing second with Upset three times, Wildair once, and John P. Grier once. He had John P. Grier ready again off two overnight victories and announced that the Dwyer was the spot— Aqueduct on June 20, 1920. It has become famous as the last challenge.

John P. Grier broke first, but Man o' War took a half-length lead after the first quarter-mile. Eddie Ambrose moved John P. Grier up on the outside and raced at Man o' War's head. The first half was run in :46, two-fifths of a second faster than the track record; the first six furlongs were run in 1:09 3/5, 1 2/5 seconds under the track standard, and John P. Grier was still there.

Then Ambrose called for John P. Grier's greatest effort, and for a moment he wrested the lead from Man o' War. Kummer drew his whip and Man o' War answered the call. The mile was raced in 1:36, two-fifths faster than the track record. Man o' War took command; John P. Grier faltered. Man o' War drew clear, winning by 1 1/2 lengths in new American-record time for 1 1/8 miles, 1:49 1/5.

Never again was Man o' War brought to such a drive. With Earl Sande up, he won the Miller Stakes, unextended, by six lengths from Donnacona. For the Travers, Rowe sent Upset and John P. Grier after him again and got no closer than 2 1/2 lengths as Andy Shuttinger eased Man o' War at the end, yet equaling Saratoga's track record for 1 1/4 miles, 2:01 4/5. For the Lawrence Realization, Mrs. Jeffords entered Hoodwink to avoid a walkover and Man o' War won by a distance arbitrarily estimated at 100 lengths. Taken under restraint in the stretch, Man o' War finished the 1 5/8 miles in 2:40 4/5, smashing Fitz Herbert's eleven-year-old American record by 4 1/5 seconds.

Next came the Jockey Club Gold Cup, which produced yet another American record, 1 1/2 miles in 2:28 4/5, a mark that stood until Man o' War's best son, War Admiral, beat it. Then came the Potomac Handicap, and he carried 138 pounds over a deep and cuppy track to set Havre de Grace's track record for 1 1/16 miles at 1:44 4/5. Wildair finished 1 1/2 lengths back in second, getting thirty pounds from the winner.

This set the stage for the final race, a meeting with four-year-old champion Sir Barton. Unfortunately, Sir Barton was not at his best, under the whip after the first quarter of a mile, and Man o' War thundered away to win the Kenilworth Gold Cup by seven lengths in 2:03, lowering the track record by 6 2/5 seconds. There was no more. He had beaten them all.

Eight of his eleven races at three had been in record times, five of them establishing new American standards, and the $80,000 purse in his final race pushed his earnings past Domino's long-standing mark to a record $249,465. Riddle asked handicapper Walter S. Vosburgh what weight Man o' War would carry if he raced at four, and Vosburgh promised it would be the highest ever assigned a Thoroughbred. Riddle quickly concluded nothing more could be proved by racing Man o' War and he was returned to Kentucky. On January 28, 1921, he was galloped once around the old Kentucky Association track in Lexington and then went to Hinata Stock Farm to the care of Miss Elizabeth Daingerfield and groom John (Buck) Buckner.

The mares selected to be bred to Man o' War were an uncommonly bad lot, undistinguished as runners or producers, so it was unreasonable to expect him to breed on his exceptional racing ability. Yet even with inferior mates, Man o' War proved to be an extraordinary success as a stallion, topping the sire list with only three crops racing, establishing a record for progeny earnings in 1926 at $408,137, far surpassing the previous record of $296,204 which had been set by his sire, Fair Play.

From Man o' War's first crop came five stakes winners, including three champions: Belmont winner American Flag, and the two best three-year-old fillies, Alabama winner Maid At Arms and Coaching Club American Oaks winner Florence Nightingale. From his second crop came six more stakes winners including two more champions, Belmont winner Crusader and Coaching Club American Oaks winner Edith Cavell. From his third crop came another six stakes winners including another champion, Futurity winner Scapa Flow. From his fourth crop came four more stakes winners including another champion filly, Suburban winner Bateau. In his fifth crop were six more stakes winners including Kentucky Derby winner Clyde Van Dusen.

From his first five crops, Man o' War sired ninety named foals, and twenty-six of them won stakes. This is 29 percent stakes winners, a phenomenal percentage of high class, as compared to the average of the breed—2.5 percent stakes winners.

In all, Man o' War sired a total of sixty-four stakes winners, nine of them champions, including Battleship, winner of the historic Aintree Grand National Steeplechase. Of all the notable sons and daughters of Man o' War, his best was War Admiral, a small bay colt sired when Big Red was well along in years.

War Admiral was an undefeated champion at three, winner of the 1937 Triple Crown, and probably the best horse in America the following year. He won ten of a dozen challenges as a handicapper, but he lost, conspicuously, the famous match race at Pimlico with Seabiscuit; this defeat was more attributable to George Woolf's artful ride on Seabiscuit than to any inferiority on the part of War Admiral, but it cost him year-end championship honors.

War Admiral was not only one of Man o' War's best racing sons but unquestionably his most successful son at stud. War Admiral topped the American sire list in 1945, when represented by champion Busher and others and subsequently became America's leading sire of broodmares in 1962 and again in 1964.

After serving two stud seasons at Hinata, Man o' War was moved up the pike to Faraway Farm where in 1930 he came under the management of Harrie B. Scott, Sr., and groom Will Harbut. Thousands of visitors to Faraway heard Harbut's gradually constructed monologue brighten the legend of Man o' War for more than fifteen years. Harbut suffered a heart attack and died October 3, 1947; Man o' War followed him within a month.

What Man o' War would have sired had he been bred to better broodmares is conjecture, of course, but it is suspected that his record as a stallion might have been more illustrious than his record as a racehorse. Such a stallion, we have yet to see.

BOLD RULER

AT THE TOP, one is subject to chary criticism. Apparently, people do not want to recognize superlative performance without qualifying it, by noting some shortcoming. Yes, Jim Brown and O. J. Simpson could carry the ball, but they could not block. Yes, Bill Russell could block shots and rebound, but he could not score. Yes, Ted Williams could hit, but he could not field.

Actually, Williams could play Fenway Park's tricky outfield like nobody's business; Russell could score anytime he thought his team needed him to shoot; and both Brown and Simpson probably could have been devastating blockers had their coaches been foolish enough to exhaust them at that task—but what does it matter, really? These were among the greatest athletes ever seen, and to deprecate their extraordinary performance is idle.

Bold Ruler suffers such slings and arrows. He was voted the best racehorse in North America in 1957, and there are those who say it was a paper title won off one race, that Bold Ruler was plain looking, unsound, and was not a real distance horse. At stud, Bold Ruler led the general sire list eight times, yet there were those who contended his success was attributable to the high-quality broodmares to which he was mated.

We shall take as a premise here that Bold Ruler was a top colt as a runner, whose innate superiority was ratified

as a stallion, and that he was one of the greatest Thoroughbreds ever foaled in Kentucky. With that, we can get on
with some of the people who had the good fortune to be
associated with him. When seeing a turtle on a fence post,
it should be remembered that he did not get there by himself.

Bold Ruler was foaled April 6, 1954, at Claiborne Farm.
Nothing nicer could happen to a horse. Claiborne is
something of an institution as Thoroughbred nurseries
go. Four generations of Hancocks have been building it
for more than a century and now have 6,000 acres outside
Paris, Kentucky, and a reputation for raising good horses
that extends considerably beyond Bourbon County, to
South America, Europe, Japan—wherever man is concerned with the running horse.

The Civil War divided, ended, and began many things
in this country. Historians, sociologists, economists have
fairly well documented how this single political eruption
changed the very lives of the born and unborn, changed
the style and manner of living, changed sources of wealth
and endeavour. The Civil War also was a benchmark in
the history of racing. In antebellum days, horse racing
was a sporting diversion of large landowners and stock
raisers, particularly in the South, with Kentucky being
known as a hotbed for enthusiasts of the sport. After the
Civil War, while Kentucky strengthened its reputation for
raising blood horses, major interest in racing centered in
New York. Purse money became significant, elaborate
racing plants were built there to accommodate an in-
creasing number of spectators. In short, racing was
changed from a rural southern sport to an urban northern
sport-business. At the time of the Civil War, racing experienced a dramatic change from a country-club sport
played by few, to a professional game played by the best
for important money and enjoyed by vast numbers of the
general public. It was just after the Civil War that the
Hancocks started raising racehorses.

Captain Richard J. Hancock, as might be suspected of a member of General Stonewall Jackson's command, was wounded three times. Toward the end of the war, Captain Hancock was wounded during a skirmish near Charlottesville, Virginia, and successfully eluded his blue-clad pursuers in the woods of Ellerslie, owned by the Harris family. From the mansion house of Ellerslie came food and medical care that kept the wounded soldier alive; and from Ellerslie, before the war ended, the captain took himself a bride, Thomasia Overton Harris, through whose inheritance, Hancock eventually became master of one of Virginia's finest estates.

Racing man T. W. Doswell drew Hancock into the Thoroughbred business. In 1871 Doswell invited Hancock to see one of his horses, Eolus, race at Pimlico in Baltimore. Hancock was enthralled. He had counted himself a good judge of horses since his childhood, when he was an enthusiastic spectator at the court-day races in North Carolina, and he saw in Eolus the marvelous conformation and spirit that he believed could be the foundation on which to build a Thoroughbred breeding operation at Ellerslie.

As often happens, his pocketbook could not match his dreams. Doswell put a price on Eolus which Hancock could not afford. Eolus consequently was sold to a Mr. Harbeck of New York, for whom Eolus proved to be a good racehorse, winning eight races before he broke down at Saratoga. Having no interest in breeding, Harbeck shipped Eolus back to Baltimore with a message for his friend, Governor Oden Bowie, to dispose of him as best he could. When Hancock learned of this turn of events, he inquired of the governor. Eolus already had been sold, and the governor could not remember who had bought him.

Hancock set about to find him, up and down the Atlantic seaboard he went, searching for the stallion named Eolus. For two years Hancock searched. Then he wrote a letter to Sanders D. Bruce, compiler of the *American Stud*

Book, and then editor of *Turf, Field and Farm*, a sporting weekly published in New York. Eolus had been sold to a farmer named Craynor who, on the Eastern Shore of Maryland, had turned Eolus into a buggy horse and found the Thoroughbred could outtrot anything in the neighborhood. Craynor ultimately forwarded to Bruce for publication in his journal a challenge to trot Eolus against any horse in Cecil County. Bruce promptly advised Hancock.

After a series of correspondence with Craynor, Hancock finally was able to strike a deal, an even trade. Doswell had given Hancock an undistinguished half-brother to Eolus named Scathelock, and Hancock traded Scathelock to Craynor for Eolus. The black groom Hancock sent to Baltimore to effect the trade was aghast when he saw Eolus, disfigured by harness galls. The boss is gonna shoot me, the groom thought, bringing this sorry horse home, but he's been wanting this horse so long, I better risk it. And a battered Eolus finally was brought through the gates of Ellerslie in 1877.

Five years earlier, Hancock had purchased his first Thoroughbred mare, War Song, by War Dance. He bred War Song to Eolus and got a colt, the only foal sired by Eolus that first year at Ellerslie. The colt was named Eole, and he became a champion, the first of many bred by the Hancock family.

Eole grew quickly into a big colt, too big and ungainly to race at two. He made his first start at three, in the classic Belmont Stakes in New York, and finished second in the all-orange silks of Doswell, with whom Hancock had become a racing partner. Later Eole was sold to Freddie Gebhard and at the ages of four and five was ranked as the best cup horse in America, winning the Great Metropolitan, Jockey Club, Monmouth, Champion, Morrissey, Autumn (twice), Coney Island, Stirrup, Great Long Island, Navesink, and Freehold stakes. As a seven-year-old, Eole was shipped to England by Gebhard, where he did not win in four starts, but finished second to champion St. Gatien in the classic Ascot Gold Cup.

Eole made Eolus a celebrated stallion, and Eolus made Ellerslie one of the most famous Thoroughbred breeding nurseries in Virginia. Bred to only a few mares, Eolus nonetheless sired a number of distinguished racers that came from Ellerslie: Knight of Ellerslie carried the Doswell-Hancock silks to victory in the 1884 Preakness; then came champion Morello, Suburban winners Eurus and Elkwood; Brooklyn Handicap winners Russell and Diavolo; Eon, Little Jim, and Charade were among the front rank of a regiment of good horses bred by Captain R. J. Hancock at Ellerslie.

In 1875 at Ellerslie, Arthur Boyd Hancock was born. When he was eleven, his father terminated his racing operation in partnership with Doswell and started offering all his Thoroughbred yearlings at public auction. From 1886 through 1953, Hancock yearlings were offered for sale. (In 1954 A.B. Hancock, Jr., decided to race some Claiborne horses in all-orange silks and to sell half his yearlings privately; in his will, he directed that his son return to the practice of selling Claiborne yearlings at public auction. After a twenty-year absence from the marketplace, the first consignment of Claiborne sale yearlings was sent to Keeneland in 1973 by young Seth Hancock; eighteen brought $2,364,000. Among these was a colt from the last crop sired by Bold Ruler; the colt was sold for a world-record price of $600,000 and emerged as the champion three-year-old of 1975—Wajima.)

In 1895 a lanky (6-foot-6, 165 pounds) young Arthur Hancock returned from the University of Chicago with letters in track and a business degree to assist his father in the management of Ellerslie. He had been working with the yearlings, taking them to New York for auctions, since he was fifteen, and while two of his brothers became practicing physicians and the other a university professor of mathematics, there never was any doubt as to the career for Arthur Hancock: He was to be a horseman.

He took over full management of the farm in 1909, three years before his father's death. He started when others were quitting. The Thoroughbred industry was at its lowest ebb in the United States. Governor Charles E. Hughes had led a reform movement which resulted in termination of racing in New York, and the sport barely survived in Kentucky and Maryland. The market for Thoroughbreds almost disappeared. Good broodmares were sold for $1,000, ordinary Thoroughbreds bringing prices only slightly above those for work horses. The broodmare band at Ellerslie was reduced to a dozen mares.

While leading Kentucky breeders—Colonel Milton Young at McGrathiana, Clay and Woodford at Runny-mede, James Ben Ali Haggin at Elmendorf Farm—dispersed their broodmares, Arthur Hancock harbored no thought of retiring from Thoroughbred breeding. "As long as I can make enough on the farm to feed those mares, I am going to keep them," he announced. It was during this unpromising period that Arthur Hancock made the first important move of his independent career. He went searching for a stallion to restore the fame of Ellerslie in the day of Eolus. He found him in Celt. A good racing son of Commando, Celt had been overshadowed on the track by his illustrious stablemate, unbeaten Colin, also by Commando. Hancock secured from James R. Keene a two-year lease on Celt as a stallion, the price to be one-third of the revenues realized by the sale of Celt yearlings. The first two crops of foals by Celt were so promising that Hancock wanted to renew the lease, but Keene did not, so at the end of the 1912 breeding season, Celt was returned to Keene's Castleton Stud in Kentucky. That year, however, Keene died and Celt was included in the estate dispersal sale in New York. Hancock bought him for $25,000 and returned Celt to the stallion barn at Ellerslie. The success of Celt, of his progeny in the sale ring and on the race track (he was America's leading sire in 1919) returned Ellerslie to the preeminent position it had held in the days of Eolus.

In 1908 Arthur Hancock married Nancy Tucker Clay of Paris, Kentucky. Two years later she inherited about 1,300 acres of the best land in Bourbon County. The couple lived at Ellerslie in Virginia, but Arthur made frequent trips to Kentucky to see that the farm was going well. After a number of these trips, he concluded that Ellerslie, well organized and with experienced help, could take better care of itself than could the new Kentucky farm, so in 1915 the Hancocks moved to Paris.

The Bluegrass farm had no name or reputation as did Ellerslie. About this time, in Fayette County, Mrs. Clarence LeBus became interested in things Japanese and decided to change the name of her farm from Claiborne to Hinata (a Japanese word for sunshine). Mrs. Hancock like the name Claiborne—it seemed to fit somehow with Clay—and adopted it, where it was to become one of the most famous names in the history of Thoroughbred breeding.

When Arthur Hancock decided to start breeding Thoroughbreds both at Ellerslie and Claiborne, he looked about for another stallion. The British Bloodstock Agency (BBA), then in its infancy, sent a photograph of a stallion of modest racing credentials in England; indeed, the horse had performed as a steeplechaser, which usually means the horse was not a good racer on the flat and consequently a poor risk as a stallion. Hancock, however, liked the looks of the horse named Wrack and bought him cheaply, for $8,000, to stand at Claiborne. Wrack was the first of many important horses sold by the BBA to American breeders, and he proved to be one of the most prolific and successful stallions of his day, ranking among America's leading sires for a dozen years.

Another significant stallion purchase by Hancock was Sir Gallahad III in 1926. Together with William Woodward, Robert A. Fairbairn, and Marshall Field, Hancock brought Sir Gallahad III from France at a cost of $125,000. From his first crop sired at Claiborne came Gallant Fox, Triple Crown winner of 1930. Sir Gallahad III was to lead America's general sire list four times and rank at the top of the list of broodmare sires for a record twelve years.

The next signal purchase of a stallion by Hancock was in 1936 when he bought Blenheim II for $250,000. Hancock formed a syndicate of seven breeders, each with undivided ownership interests in the stallion, to buy Blenheim II. From his first crop sired at Claiborne came Whirlaway, Triple Crown winner of 1941. Blenheim II, which also led both the general sire list and broodmare sire list, was the forerunner of a system of multiple ownership of expensive stallions which became common practice after World War II. Syndication permitted prices for stallion prospects to rise from Nashua's $1,251,200 price to the $7.2 million valuation placed on the thirty-six-share Wajima syndicate.

While Wrack, then Sir Gallahad III and Blenheim II, headed the Claiborne stallion roster, many other celebrated racers were retired to stud there, and the Hancock broodmare band grew to more than a hundred mares. Foals bred at Claiborne were offered at auction as yearlings, and their subsequent racing success placed Hancock's name at the top of the list of America's breeders in races won nine times (1935–1938, 1940, 1942–1944, 1946) and in purses earned five times (1935–1937, 1939, 1943). He succeeded John E. Madden as America's most prominent commercial breeder, sending out 138 stakes winners, including nine champions— Cleopatra, Careful, St. James, Nimba, Current, Tintagel, Forever Yours, Jacola, and Beaugay—plus other top horses such as Dunboyne, Polka Dot, Vigil, Gallant Sir, Hadagal, Calumet Dick, Reaping Reward, Sky Larking, Slide Rule, Whirlabout, Stir Up, Fighting Frank, and Kentucky Derby winners Johnstown and Jet Pilot.

Arthur Hancock served as president of the old Thoroughbred Horse Association. He was instrumental in famous vendue in 1917. He was a founder of the Breeders Sales Company in Lexington in 1943. He was one of the original three voting trustees of the Keeneland Association. He was a member of the Kentucky State Racing Commission. In 1944 he was honored by the Thoroughbred Club of America with a testimonial dinner for his special contributions to the Thoroughbred industry.

The success of Arthur Hancock in breeding good horses for nearly four decades attracted clients, wealthy easterners who preferred to breed their racers rather than buy yearlings, but who did not wish to become involved in the details of farm operations—clients such as banker William Woodward, publisher Marshall Field, Wall Street broker Robert Fairbairn, industrialist Harry Guggenheim, utilities magnate Christopher T. Chenery, and the Phipps family.

About the time of the Civil War, a young Andrew Carnegie came upon an opportunity to buy the Kloman forge at Girty's Run near Pittsburgh. He went to a young accountant friend, Henry Phipps, and let him in for half the deal, for $800 and the responsibility of keeping the books. This company in turn became known as the Carnegie Steel Company and thirty-eight years later, United States Steel, when J. P. Morgan turned over a handsome check to the partners. On his $800 investment, Henry Phipps realized $50 million.

Phipps's son, Henry Carnegie Phipps, married Gladys Livingston Mills, and thereby merged two of America's great fortunes. On her mother's side, Gladys Mills descended from the Livingstons who acted as Indian Affairs agents for the British Crown, signed the Declaration of Independence, ran New York and New Jersey politics, held the monopoly on steamboating on the Hudson, handled the Louisiana Purchase, and were among the largest real estate owners in America. Gladys Mills's grandfather, Darius Ogden Mills, accumulated considerable wealth in California after the Gold Rush, as a banker and merchant prince, and increased that fortune in New York on Wall Street and with hotels and other real estate investments. D. O. Mills's grandson, Ogden Livingston Mills, became secretary of the treasury under Herbert Hoover. Ogden Livingston Mills's twin sisters, Gladys and Beatrice, were both interested in horses. Beatrice moved to En-gland where, as Countess Granard, she raced some horses in partnership with Lord Derby, won the 1933 Grand Prix de Paris with Cappiello, and bred and raced a colt sired by her sister's stallion Bold Ruler; named Bold Lad, the colt became the champion two-year-old of 1966 in England.

The Wheatley Stable was formed in the 1920s by Mrs. H. C. Phipps with her husband, who was more interested in Wall Street and high-stakes poker, and her brother Ogden L. Mills, who was more interested in Wall Street and politics, a form of high-stakes poker. According to legend, the making of Wheatley Stable came out of a poker game. Harry Payne Whitney had inherited a good deal of New York Transit, Standard Oil, American Tobacco, and a love of Thoroughbreds—a small part of which he lost to Henry Carnegie Phipps one night at the poker table. At the time, Whitney was the only man in America who had bred more stakes winners than Arthur Hancock, and Whitney offered to pay off his gambling debt to Phipps by giving him his pick of the Whitney yearlings. This mode of payment was not without design, for Phipps knew or cared little about horses. The following morning, however, Phipps showed up at Whitney's Brookdale Farm in New Jersey with his wife, a person who was very knowledgeable about horses. Among the yearlings she picked were Dice, sensational unbeaten two-year-old of 1927; distinguished cup horse Diavolo, handicap champion of 1929; and another stakes winner, Distraction. Thus it could be said that from the beginning, success of Wheatley Stable was in the cards.

Following the death of her brother, and then of her husband, Mrs. H. C. Phipps continued to operate Wheatley Stable until her death in 1970 at the age of eighty-seven. From a relatively small number of mares kept with the Hancocks at Claiborne, Mrs. Phipps's Wheatley Stable bred a succession of stakes winners, ninety-four in all, of which eleven were voted champions: Seabiscuit (which Wheatley sold as a three-year-old and later became the world's leading money earner), High Voltage, Misty Morn, Bold Ruler, Castle Forbes, Bold Lad, Queen Empress, Bold Bidder, Successor, Top Bid, and Autobiography.

Mrs. Phipps's children also boarded their Thoroughbred mares at Claiborne. Her daughter, Mrs. Stuart Janney, at Claiborne bred 1974–1975 champion Ruffian. Her son, Ogden Phipps, former chairman of The Jockey Club, at Claiborne bred mighty Buckpasser, 1966 Horse of the Year which now stands at Claiborne. Other grandchildren of Andrew Carnegie's partner, John Phipps, who have left the breeding and raising of their Thoroughbreds to the Hancocks include polo players Mike and Hubert Phipps, Winston and Raymond Guest. The latter, former United States Ambassador to Ireland, now stands his former race champions Tom Rolfe and Sir Ivor at Claiborne.

In 1910 A. B. Hancock, Jr., was born in his uncle's house, Marchmont (now a part of Claiborne and the residence of young Seth Hancock). He attended public school in Paris, Kentucky, until he was thirteen and was sent to Saint Marks. He complained to his father, "There isn't a *Daily Racing Form* within a hundred miles of Southboro, Mass." and thus was transferred to Woodberry Forest in Virginia. Indeed, how could a young horseman be expected to receive a proper education without access to the most essential of reference journals? From Woodberry, young Hancock picked up the nickname of Bull, which he carried on to Princeton and throughout his life. In 1933 Bull Hancock returned from

141

Princeton with numerals in baseball and football and a degree with a major in eugenics to assist his father in the management of Claiborne.

This was a step up from his summer jobs, raking barn hallways and mucking out yearlings' stalls at fifty cents a day. The first year he was placed in charge of the brood-mares, the next year in charge of the yearlings. In 1937 he was placed in charge of Ellerslie.

"The first year I was over there, the farm showed a profit of $2,000 and I was quite pleased. The next year it lost $15,000 and I didn't know how to tell my father. But he said not to worry about it; he'd been trying for 30 years, he said, and could not make a go of it." During the 1920s and 1930s, the Hancocks' attention and emphasis was shifted from Ellerslie to Claiborne, where the highest number and most valuable mares and stallions were quartered. In 1946 Ellerslie was sold, and all the horses were moved to Claiborne.

Discharged from the Army Air Corps as a captain in 1945, when his father suffered the first of a series of heart attacks, Bull Hancock returned to Claiborne and found almost the same situation which had faced his father when he had taken over management from an ailing Captain Richard Hancock forty years earlier: A great horse breeding establishment had grown old. The Claiborne stallion roster still was headed by Blenheim II, past his prime at eighteen; four-time leading sire Sir Gallahad III was twenty-five; the other stallions never were to prove successful; some 250 mares were on the place and as a group they were old, had distinguished relatives, but had done little to distinguish themselves. A restocking, revitalization of farm operation was in order. As the elder Hancock's health declined, Bull Hancock assumed more responsibility and took over complete management when Arthur Hancock, Sr., suffered a stroke in 1947.

As had his grandfather with Eolus and his father with Celt, Bull Hancock built success on a foundation of stallions. The first stallion Bull Hancock selected was Princequillo, an outstanding cup horse. No one, apparently, thought Princequillo would amount to much as a stallion and he attracted only a few mares at his modest stud fee of $250. Among the farm clients whose mares were bred to Princequillo that first year in 1945 were William Woodward and Chris Chenery. Woodward's mare produced Prince Simon, top-ranked three-year-old in England, while Chenery's mare produced Hill Prince, voted champion in America at two and three. Thereafter no question remained as to the merit of Princequillo, sire of numerous champions (including Claiborne-bred Round Table) and America's leading sire in 1957–1958. The second stallion which Bull Hancock brought to Claiborne was Ambiorix, a champion two-year-old in France which was purchased for $250,000, quickly syndicated, and which became America's leading stallion in 1961.

"What I wanted, though, was a Nearco stallion," recalled Bull Hancock. "There was only one in America at the time, and he had not been anything as a racehorse, and was of no consequence as a stallion. I liked Nasrullah because he was the top ranked two-year-old colt in England in 1942, and an unlucky third in the English Derby. I had the British Bloodstock Agency offer $50,000 for him when he was in training, but his owner, the Aga Khan, had sold him a week earlier. Then I thought I had him bought later, for 100,000 pounds, but the deal fell through when the pound was devalued. The next year, in December of 1949, we bought him for $340,000." The buyers were Hancock and farm clients William Woodward and Harry Guggenheim. Nasrullah was quickly syndicated into thirty-two shares of ownership.

Nasrullah was a more important purchase than that of leading sires Blenheim II or Sir Gallahad III or Celt. The purchase of Nasrullah not only turned around the fortunes of Claiborne, it affected the entire Thoroughbred industry in America. Nasrullah, whose English progeny had placed him at the top of England's sire list in 1951, was to head America's sire list five times from 1955

143

through 1962. His son Bold Ruler was to lead America's sires eight times from 1963 through 1973; and Bold Ruler's son What a Pleasure topped the sire lists in 1975. Nasrullah sired a record ninety-nine stakes winners here and abroad; the stallion with the second-greatest number of stakes winners is Bold Ruler with eighty. Quite probably, Nasrullah was the most influential, the most important stallion imported to America since the first English Derby winner, Diomed, arrived in Virginia in 1800.

Of nine American champions sired by Nasrullah, the first foaled at Claiborne was Nashua. He was bred by William Woodward, Sr., and was raced after his breeder's death in 1953 by William Woodward, Jr. The latter was accidentally killed by his wife in 1955, and three-year-old Nashua, then Horse of the Year, was auctioned by the estate by means of sealed bids. Leslie Combs II submitted the winning bid of $1,251,200 on behalf of a syndicate. It marked the first time a horse ever had been sold for as much as one million dollars. Nashua continued to race as a four-year-old, in the colors of Combs, and was retired as the world's greatest money earner with $1,288,565.

Nashua was trained by Sunny Jim Fitzsimmons who, literally, was born and raised on the race tracks. Over a seventy-year period, he had seen the promise of many horses and had developed an extraordinary number, 149, to win major stakes; nearly all of these had been foaled and raised at Claiborne Farm. From Claiborne, Woodward had sent him Sir Gallahad III's son Gallant Fox, which Sunny Jim had trained to win the Kentucky Derby, Preakness, and Belmont Stakes to become America's greatest money earner; from Claiborne, Woodward sent him Gallant Fox's son Omaha, which Sunny Jim also trained to win the Kentucky Derby, Preakness, and Belmont; there followed Kentucky Derby winners Granville and Johnstown, filly champions Happy Gal and Vagrancy; the last Woodward champion from Claiborne was Nashua, by Nasrullah.

144

Mrs. H. C. Phipps
leads into the winner's
circle her most
famous champion,
Bold Ruler, ridden
by Eddie Arcaro.
*(New York Racing
Association)*

Arthur B. Hancock, Sr.

A. B. (Bull) Hancock, Jr.

When Nashua was four, Sunny Jim had in his barn another Nasrullah colt, a two-year-old destined to be a champion—Wheatley Stable's Bold Ruler. He had not impressed Bull Hancock as a foal, "He was very skinny with a large hernia. We had the devil's own time trying to get him to look good, and I must say, I never was really pleased with his condition the whole time I had him." Throughout his racing career, Bold Ruler was hampered by a chronic rheumatic condition and never was completely sound. He suffered a tongue injury as a yearling, which probably accounted for his never wanting a rider to pull on his mouth so as to rate his speed during the early part of his races. Twice he was injured in starting gates and his two-year-old campaign was interrupted by a pulled back muscle and a hock injury.

Despite his physical problems, Bold Ruler won his first five races and he was recognized as the season's leading two-year-old. Then he suffered his first defeat, in an allowance race won by Nashville, another son of Nasrullah. Sunny Jim brought him back, however, to win the historic Futurity on the same day four-year-old Nashua won the Jockey Club Gold Cup in American-record time, for his last appearance on the Turf. Bold Ruler raced twice more that season and lost the division championship because of these performances. In the Garden State Stakes, he ran onto the heels of the pacemaker and then dropped back out of the running to finish unplaced. In the Remsen, he got off to a poor start, was forced to the outside on the first turn, and would not make any further effort. The Garden State Stakes winner, Barbizon was voted champion, and Bold Ruler, with seven victories in ten starts, was ranked second on the Experimental Free Handicap at the conclusion of the season.

At three, Bold Ruler began by winning the seven-furlong Bahamas Stakes in Florida, defeating Calumet Farm's brilliant Gen. Duke in time that equaled the track record. Next, in the nine-furlong Everglades Stakes, he conceded twelve pounds to Gen. Duke and was beaten by a head, but in the nine-furlong Flamingo Stakes, at level weights with Gen. Duke, Bold Ruler won by a neck and lowered the track record for nine furlongs to 1:47. The next encounter of the two rivals came in the nine-furlong Florida Derby, at equal weights, and Gen. Duke won by 1 1/2 lengths from Bold Ruler, in 1:46 4/5, time that equaled the world record for the distance. At this point, it appeared that Bold Ruler and Gen. Duke were of equal ability; Gen. Duke, however, developed a spinal disease that caused him to be scratched from the Kentucky Derby on the eve of the race for which he was favored, and he never raced again.

Meanwhile, Bold Ruler had found another rival en route to the Kentucky Derby, Gallant Man, which Bold Ruler managed to defeat by a nose margin in the Wood Memorial. With Gen. Duke declared from the race, Bold Ruler was installed as the betting choice for the Kentucky Derby. His rider, Eddie Arcaro, figured the horse to beat was Gallant Man, and he attempted to rate Bold Ruler during the early part of the race to save something for the late challenge that was certain to come from Gallant Man. Bold Ruler fought Arcaro's attempt to hold him back during the early running and had nothing left for the stretch run. Gallant Man rushed by in the stretch, taking aim on the leader, Iron Liege, a stablemate of the ill-fated Gen. Duke. Gallant Man's rider, Bill Shoemaker, misjudged the finish line, rising in his stirrups at the sixteenth pole; it was only a moment's hesitation, but just enough to cause Gallant Man to lose to Iron Liege by a nose margin. Behind Gallant Man came Round Table, a Princequillo colt bred by Hancock and foaled at Claiborne the same day as was Bold Ruler. Fourth was Bold Ruler.

In the Preakness, Arcaro let Bold Ruler run freely, and he easily defeated Iron Liege. In the 1 1/2-mile Belmont Stakes, however, Bold Ruler led for the first 1 1/4 miles in a fast 2:01 2/5, but he had no strength left to withstand the closing rush of Gallant Man, which hurried by to win by

147

twelve lengths in new American time for 1 1/2 miles of 2:26 3/5. Bold Ruler was given a three-month rest. Meanwhile, Gallant Man reigned as the best three-year-old in the East, Round Table the best in the West with a remarkable series of victories in California.

Bold Ruler was brought back in September and won two races, then finished third in the Woodward Stakes to older Dedicate and Gallant Man. Next he won the seven-furlong Vosburgh in record time, carried 133 pounds in the Queens County against older horses and won, and carried a monstrous 136 pounds in the Benjamin Franklin and won by twelve lengths. These performances indicated he was ready to challenge the division leaders, Gallant Man and Round Table; the opportunity arose in the 1 1/4-mile Trenton Handicap at Garden State Park on November 9. It was the most important race of the year, for it decided the championship. The handicapper assigned Gallant Man and Round Table equal high weight of 124 pounds, Bold Ruler two pounds less; the betting public installed Gallant Man a slight favorite at $2.80–2, Bold Ruler second choice at $3.20–2.

It has been said that Eddie Arcaro won this race. Bold Ruler had failed in his only attempts at distances as great as 1 1/4 miles, finishing fourth in the Kentucky Derby, third in the Belmont, and third in the Woodward. Gallant Man and Round Table both had performed well in distance races. Arcaro sent Bold Ruler winging to an early lead in the Trenton, opening a margin as great as eight lengths at one point. It was thought that Bold Ruler would tire after a mile or so, and the issue would be met in the stretch with Gallant Man and Round Table. While these tarried in the early running, however, Arcaro had Bold Ruler running easily on the lead; turning for home, Arcaro merely showed Bold Ruler the whip, never once struck the horse, and Bold Ruler galloped on, winning by 2 1/4 lengths from Gallant Man, with Round Table third. Bold Ruler was voted champion three-year-old colt and Horse of the Year.

At four, Bold Ruler proved to be a superior weight carrier. He won the six-furlong Toboggan with 133 pounds, the seven-furlong Carter with 135 (giving seven pounds to Gallant Man, which finished third), then lost the Metropolitan Mile to Gallant Man, which carried 130 pounds to Bold Ruler's 135.

Bold Ruler then won the 1 1/8-mile Stymie with 133 pounds and next captured the historic 1 1/4-mile Suburban Handicap with a 134-pound burden. He won the 1 1/4-mile Monmouth Handicap also with 134 pounds, but in attempting to carry 136 pounds a week later in the Brooklyn, Bold Ruler broke down. He never raced again. He had won twenty-three of his thirty-three races and had earned $764,204. His brilliant performances up until July were overshadowed in the fall by those of Round Table, which that season surpassed Nashua's earnings mark to become the world's greatest money earner. Round Table was voted Horse of the Year, and Bold Ruler as champion sprinter for 1958. Bold Ruler was returned to Claiborne to begin his career as a stallion under the management of Bull Hancock.

Bold Ruler joined a distinguished stallion roster that Bull Hancock had selected for Claiborne. Selecting a stallion is at once the most difficult and most important of factors for success in the horse-breeding business. Bull Hancock was better at it than any man who came before him.

One of the reasons it is difficult to pick a stallion is that only a dozen out of every 10,000 registered Thoroughbred colts ever prove to be successful as stallions. A measure of success is the Average-Earnings Index, a ratio of the earnings of racing progeny sired by one stallion compared to the average earnings of all racehorses. An Average-Earnings Index of 1.00 indicates a stallion's progeny earned the same amount of purse money as the average of all horses; an Average-Earnings Index of 2.00 indicates a stallion's progeny earned twice as much as the average. Only 5 percent of all stallions have an Average-

Earnings Index of 2.00 or higher, and these are regarded as successful stallions.

Among those few colts that have an Average-Earnings Index of 2.00 or higher and are termed successful, only one or two ever become the leading sire for a year. Stallions that Bull Hancock selected to stand at Claiborne Farm became the leading sire seventeen times from 1955 through 1973: Nasrullah led for five years, Princequillo for two, Ambiorix once, Round Table once, and Bold Ruler for eight years. While most of the 350 mares on Claiborne were owned by some forty farm clients, Bull Hancock owned about fifty, and from these Hancock bred (and sold some) runners which placed Claiborne back on top of the list of America's breeders four times, in 1958, 1959, 1968, and 1969.

For sixty-eight years the Hancock family had been selling the farm produce as yearlings. In 1954 Bull Hancock decided to take his homebreds to the race track. From that first crop of Claiborne horses to carry the all-orange silks that Knight of Ellerslie had flashed to victory in the 1884 Preakness came good fillies Delta and Courtesy. The next crop included champion filly Doubledogdare; the next, champions Round Table and Bayou.

"I would sell enough of them to pay the farm operation, then race what was left. When Round Table came along, I had him priced at $40,000 as a yearling and had a lot of lookers, but, thank goodness, no takers, so I raced him at two and he showed something. In Florida early in his 3-year-old year, I sold him for $140,000 to Travis Kerr and retained a quarter interest in him as a stallion. The sale of that horse more or less held the farm together, so we could pay the estate taxes and so on." Arthur Hancock, Sr., had died in April of 1957.

From 1952 through 1972 at Claiborne, Bull Hancock bred 101 stakes winners including ten champions— Doubledogdare, Round Table, Bayou, Nadir, Lamb Chop, Moccasin, Gamely, Thatch, Apalachee, and Wajima. Thirty-two other champions were foaled at Claiborne, raised under his supervision, and raced for farm clients. He became president of the American Thorough-bred Breeders Association, succeeded his father as a member of the Kentucky State Racing Commission and board member of Keeneland Race Course, and was an honor guest of the Thoroughbred Club of America's testimonial dinner. In 1955 he was elected to The Jockey Club as the first working horseman to become a member of that New York group of wealthy racing enthusiasts.

At Claiborne, Bold Ruler became the most successful native stallion since Lexington. America's leading sire eight times, leading sire of two-year-olds six times, Bold Ruler sired racing progeny which earned nearly eight times the average. His breeding services were priceless. Nominations to him could not be purchased for any price. An arrangement was made, however, for mares other than those owned by the Phipps family to be bred to him. Top broodmares approved by Ogden Phipps and Bull Hancock could be bred to Bold Ruler for no cash consideration, but with the provision that of the first two foals sired by Bold Ruler from those mares, one would go to Mrs. Phipps and one to the owner of the mares; ownership of the foals were to be decided by a flip of the coin. Under this arrangement, Chris Chenery in 1968-1969 sent his grand producer, Somethingroyal, by Princequillo, to the court of Bold Ruler; in 1969 Somethingroyal foaled a filly, which went to Mrs. Phipps on a coin toss. The next year Somethingroyal foaled a chestnut colt at Chenery's Meadow Stud in Virginia, not far from Ellerslie. The colt was to be named Secretariat.

That year, 1970, Bold Ruler was sixteen and in July it was noticed that he began having difficulty breathing. In August, Dr. Art Davidson strapped Bold Ruler to an operating table in his veterinary surgery hospital near Lexington and placed the stallion under general anesthesia. Dr. Davidson found a tumorous mass in the nasal passage, just below a portion of the brain. It proved to be a malignant cancer. Bold Ruler was taken by van to the veterinary school at Auburn University where the tumor, which grew to the size of a tennis ball, was arrested with cobalt treatments administered by Auburn veterinary scientists in consultation with specialists who had treated similar malignancies in humans. Bold Ruler responded well to the treatments, was returned to Claiborne in October, regained lost weight, and seemed to return to his old vigor. In the spring of 1971, he was bred to thirty-seven mares and from these sired twenty-three foals in his last crop. During June, Bold Ruler, although continuing to clean up his feed tub, began to lose weight again. He showed a loss of vigor. On July 2 a biopsy of tissue taken from his neck confirmed that the cancer had reappeared; a new, relentless onslaught had produced tumors and lesions inside the head, neck, and chest. Bold Ruler was put down at Claiborne on July 12, 1971.

Of the many legacies Bold Ruler left to the Turf, his greatest was a chestnut yearling romping in a paddock at The Meadow in Virginia. This was Secretariat. Here was one to stir an Emerson: Born for success he seemed, with grace to win, heart to hold, and shining gifts that take all eyes. Highly bred, impressive in appearance, spectacular in performance, Secretariat was the personification of a dream, dreamed by all men who would look upon greatness in a Thoroughbred and say, ah, that he came along in our time.

Secretariat was trained by Lucien Laurin, a French-Canadian and former jockey who once trained for Bull Hancock. For Chenery's Meadow Stable he saddled Claiborne-foaled Riva Ridge, champion two-year-old of 1971 and winner of the Kentucky Derby and Belmont Stakes in 1972, when Secretariat was two. Secretariat unexpectedly lost his first race; he was slammed at the start and finished fourth. He was to finish other than first on three other occasions during his racing career—each time unexpectedly, for there was nothing about Secretariat that prompted doubt of victory.

Secretariat never bounded away from the gate, in the flash of Hindoo or the power of Man o' War that devastated their rivals from the onset. Secretariat at two was content to leave the gate in a leisurely manner, settle into stride, then smash his opposition on the final turn and run away in the stretch. He won two minor purses, then the Sanford Stakes by three lengths, the historic Hopeful by five lengths, the rich Futurity by a handy 1 3/4 lengths. In the Champagne, he bullied his way to the front, seriously interfering with Stop the Music, and although Secretariat won by two lengths, the stewards disqualified him for bumping and placed him second. For that, he won the Laurel Futurity by eight lengths from Stop the Music. Secretariat then concluded the season with a smashing triumph in the rich Garden State Stakes. With seven official victories in nine starts, and earnings of $456,404, Secretariat clearly was the champion two-year-old of 1972. No juvenile had been widely recognized as better than his elders and accepted as the best horse in training since unbeaten Colin, a two-year-old of 1907; Secretariat was a unanimous selection over older champions as Horse of the Year.

Since trainer Ben Jones started the trend in 1938 of racing three-year-olds in Florida in preparation for the Kentucky Derby, the usual practice was to take a serious Kentucky Derby candidate to Florida or California. Laurin, who had prepared Riva Ridge in Florida, did not race Secretariat during the winter; he did not start Secretariat at three until he was returned to New York in March. Secretariat began with a victory in the seven-furlong Bay Shore; three weeks later he won the Gotham Mile. Then, unexpectedly, Secretariat came up with no run at all in the 1 1/8-mile Wood Memorial and finished third, four lengths behind Angle Light and Sham. The performance lent false hopes to rivals, particularly to the trainer of Sham, which had demonstrated quality in winning the Santa Catalina and Santa Anita Derby earlier in California.

In the Kentucky Derby, Secretariat was absolutely last coming down the stretch the first time, but he steadily began picking up horses on the first turn and methodically closed a ten-length margin on the leaders. Rounding the last turn, he caught Sham and the two forged into the stretch, matching strides. Secretariat pulled away at the eighth pole and won by 2 1/4 lengths. Time for the 1 1/4 miles was a sensational 1:59 2/5, the fastest Kentucky Derby ever run, eclipsing Northern Dancer's mark by three-fifths of a second.

In the next town, Baltimore, Sham's connections were still confident, but less assertive about their chances of beating Secretariat in the Preakness. Last again the first time through the stretch, jockey Ron Turcotte decided to let Secretariat run loose around the first turn, and swoosh! Without the slightest urging, Secretariat sprinted around the entire field on the first turn, spurting from last to first by the time the field straightened out for the run down the backstretch. Secretariat just coasted from there, defeating Sham by 2 1/2 lengths, again in spectacular time. Dispute arose as to how spectacular this was, for the electronic timer malfunctioned; veteran clockers timed Secretariat in 1:53 2/5, a new track record for 1 3/16 miles, but the official track timer clocked the race a second slower, two-fifths of a second slower than Canonero II's Preakness record.

Secretariat's Belmont Stakes has been characterized as the greatest performance ever seen on an American race track. He set a world record for 1 1/2 miles, lowering the Belmont Stakes record Gallant Man had set, when he defeated Bold Ruler, by more than two seconds, to 2:24 flat. But it was the manner in which he did it, with such power, such style. Whereas he was long in coming from last place to the lead in the Kentucky Derby, quick in spurting from last place to the lead in the Preakness,

Secretariat broke alertly with the leaders in the Belmont Stakes. Sprinting to an early lead has cost many champions victory in a distance race; Secretariat hurried to the front, took command entering the first turn. Obviously he was going too fast to stay, the first quarter in :23 3/5, the half-mile in :46 1/5, the first three quarters in 1:09 4/5. No horse could last 1 1/2 miles at that pace! Yet Secretariat galloped on at breakneck speed, drawing off from his rivals by seven lengths with a mile in 1:34 1/5. No horse ever had won the Belmont Stakes with such fast time for the first mile. Secretariat continued to draw away, by twenty lengths, with 1 1/4 miles in 1:59! Surely he must stop. But he did not. Without a touch of the whip, Secretariat cruised home, distancing his field, leaving his closest rival thirty-one lengths behind, galloping majestically to the thunderous applause for America's first Triple Crown winner in a quarter-century.

After Secretariat's Belmont, all was anticlimax. He was taken to Chicago for a special race, won easily by nine lengths in record time. At Saratoga, his followers were stunned by his second-place finish to an ordinary horse named Onion. Six weeks later he ratified his greatness.

In the Marlboro Cup, three-year-old Secretariat was asked to concede weight to horses the quality of which was never matched by challengers to earlier greats Sysonby, Colin, Man o' War, Citation, or Kelso. Arrayed against Secretariat were four older champions: Riva Ridge, Cougar II, Key to the Mint, and Kennedy Road. Rounding out the illustrious field were Travers winner Annihilate 'em, and Secretariat's nemesis in the Whitney Stakes, Onion. Onion set the early pace, until overtaken after a half-mile by Secretariat's stablemate, Riva Ridge. Coming from sixth place, Secretariat moved gradually toward the leaders, caught Riva Ridge on the last turn, and after a mile in a scintillating 1:33, drew off from the older champion to win by 3 1/2 lengths, champion Cougar II finishing third behind Riva Ridge. Time for the 1 1/8 miles was a world record 1:45 2/5.

He raced three more times, turning in a lackluster performance in finishing second to older Prove Out in the Woodward, then winning the Man o' War Stakes on grass, setting a new course record, and concluding with an easy victory in the Canadian International Championship. He had won sixteen of his twenty-one races, earning $1,316,808, was voted Horse of the Year again. There was nothing more to prove on the race track. He was sent to Claiborne to begin stud duty.

Bull Hancock died in September of 1972 and the management of the world's largest and most important Thoroughbred breeding establishment was thrust upon his twenty-six-year-old son Seth. Chris Chenery, who had been in ill health for several years, died in January of 1973, and management of Meadow Stud, and Secretariat, passed to his daughter, Helen C. Tweedy. To pay estate taxes, Mrs. Tweedy elected to syndicate Secretariat as a stallion before he even raced at three. She called on Seth Hancock to do the job.

His father had put together many important syndications for Claiborne stallions. In July of 1967 Bull Hancock had sold sixteen syndicate shares in champion Buckpasser for a record $150,000 a share. In August of 1970 he had sold twenty-two syndicate shares in English Triple Crown winner Nijinsky II for a new-record $170,000 a share. The price per share for Secretariat was set at $190,000, and in a matter of days, young Seth Hancock completed the syndication with the sale of twenty-eight shares. Six months later, he sold thirty syndicate shares in Riva Ridge for $160,000 each.

And thus, an institution continued. A fourth-generation Hancock picked it up. To an inheritance of land, horsemanship, reputation, Seth Hancock began in accordance with family tradition.

KENTUCKY

H ENRY CLAY was a racing man, who ran three times for the presidency of the United States. He placed twice, was out of the money once, and was on the also-eligible list several times during his forty years in the vortex of national politics.

"I would rather be right, than President," Clay rationalized. His political foes pointed out that he had no option on the matter, that he could be neither. He served, however, as Speaker of the House for thirteen years, as a senator from Kentucky for seventeen years, as secretary of state for four years, as a commissioner to Ghent to end the War of 1812, as "the great pacificator" in forging the Compromises of 1820, of 1833, of 1850.

In 1799 at the age of twenty-two, Clay moved from Virginia to Kentucky, married into a prominent Lexington family, and engaged in what he characterized as a "lucrative law practice," for in the new state the land was rich—and fertile in title disputes. Quick witted, eloquent, charming, and ambitious, he also was hot tempered and acerbic. Tall and angular, a man who appreciated fine whiskey and loved to gamble, he was regarded as the quintessential early Kentuckian. By the time he was thirty-four he had been elected to the Kentucky legislature seven times, had acquired 600 acres at the east end of Main Street in Lexington that he named Ashland Stud, had fought his first duel, had twice served in the United States Senate, had registered his racing colors of buff and blue with the Lexington Jockey Club, and was in Washington serving his first term as House Speaker.

Politics was Henry Clay's life, the practice of law (with Leslie Combs I) his means of support, and farming his hobby. The latter commanded his close attention between then-short congressional sessions. He personally supervised the cultivation of hemp, rye, and corn and the raising of mules and Arabian horses. He was the first to import Hereford cattle to America. The Lexington races were run over Clay's track at Ashland Stud in the 1820s. He was a friend of Colonel William R. Johnson and a frequent visitor at Oaklands, residence of the Napoleon of the Turf, during the race meetings at Richmond, Virginia. He frequently was invited to serve as a steward for races in Maryland, Charleston, and New Orleans.

Still, his reputation as a racing man and his reputation as the next president may have been overblown. There is no record of his colors ever being carried to victory in a significant race. He did not begin to breed race horses until 1830. In his Lexington residence, built from a design by Benjamin Latrobe (Thomas Jefferson's selection as the architect to rebuild the burned-out White House and Capitol, the man who revived Greek Revival architecture in America with the Bank of Pennsylvania in Philadelphia), Clay wrote in his farm journal the pedigree and description of his first broodmare, Susan, by the Darnaby Diomed. On the opposite page he penned, "She has a bay filly with the following marks: ————. It was foaled in the spring of 1831, and was got by Dr. Thornton's celebrated Rattler. She has also a sorrel colt foaled in the spring of 1832, with the following marks: ————." Clay never did get around to taking those markings, for he was busy that

158

year running for president again against Andrew Jackson. The latter, subsequently characterized by historian John Hervey as the Father of the Tennessee Turf, at the time was labeled "a cock-fighter, horse-racer, gambler, and brawler."

The next year, President Jackson had his race horses in the White House stable, and Clay was back breeding Thoroughbreds at Ashland, recording: "Kate, by Tiger has by her side a mare colt [an anomaly now, a filly foal then], a dark bay with a star in its forehead and left forefoot white, foaled the 5th day of May, 1833; got by Sea Gull, a celebrated Archy stud." And for a "horse colt" foaled two weeks later, out of Nancy Peters, by Sir Peter Teazle, "the colt by Sidi Hamet is a bright bay horse colt with star in its face, left hind foot white, left forefoot likewise, the hoof and the fetlock behind also white."

The last entry written in Clay's hand in the Ashland Stud journal was for a bay colt by Monarch, foaled on May 5, 1842. Thereafter, the Thoroughbred breeding operation at Ashland and its bookkeeping were turned over to his twenty-one-year-old son, John M. Clay. As a chronic presidential candidate, Henry Clay was a ready donee, and many of these gifts were horses. In 1845, shortly after losing narrowly to James Polk (50.8 percent of the popular vote to Clay's 49.2 percent), Clay accepted three magnificent gifts. From South Carolina Governor Wade Hampton II: "The bay filly Margaret Wood (by leading sire Priam) in my stable seemed to strike your fancy, so I venture to send her to you as a token of my regard. My only regret is that the offering is not worthy of your acceptance, or of the feelings that prompt me to send her." From Commodore Charles W. Morgan came the imported stallion Yorkshire, which at Ashland Stud was to rank among the ten leading sires for eight years. From a New Orleans admirer, Dr. W. N. Mercer, came Magnolia, by leading sire Glencoe.

There were others, but these three alone were the bases of the extraordinary success in Thoroughbred breeding by Henry Clay's sons and grandsons for the next forty years. Margaret Wood, a half-sister to champion four-miler Wagner, won important stakes herself and produced six stakes winners, including Star Davis. The latter sired 1878 Kentucky Derby winner Day Star, bred by John Clay. Margaret Wood was the fourth dam of 1884 American Derby winner Modesty, fourth dam of 1890 Kentucky Derby winner Riley, sixth dam of 1892 Kentucky Derby winner Azra, and seventh dam of 1896 Kentucky Derby winner Ben Brush.

Magnolia, styled by Hervey as the "Empress of the Stud Book," produced thirteen foals, all distinguished performers. Among them was Madeline, dam of Maggie B. B., from which came 1881 English Derby winner Iroquois, champions Harold, Panique, Sir Dixon, Belvidere, Sallie McClelland, and others. Madeline was by Boston. John Clay bred Magnolia to Boston's great son, Lexington, and got Kentucky, the best horse in New York for three seasons, winner of the first Travers Stakes, winner of the first two runnings of the Saratoga Cup.

John Clay was graduated from Princeton, studied for the law, but never practiced. He was said to be highly intelligent, but he had his emotional ups and downs, and was a frequent inmate of the Kentucky Lunatic Asylum, where his brother Theodore died after many years as a patient. He shied from the public limelight his father and brothers sought, devoted his life to agricultural pursuits, was well versed in pedigrees, and raised an exceptional number of good horses which he raced with considerable success for twenty years. "While to many, Mr. Clay appeared eccentric in his ways, he was a gentleman in every sense of the word, a man of scholarly attainments and refinements," noted the *Thoroughbred Record*. "He rather underrated the merits of his horses. Those who knew his peculiarities preferred buying a horse from him than anyone else, as they never left him without knowing every defect, actual or imaginary, the horse possessed."

Well, he sold Kentucky as a three-year-old, together with a good filly, Arcola, to John Hunter for only $6,000. This was in 1864, toward the end of the Civil War, when Clay decided to retire from racing. John Hunt Morgan, member of the same Lexington clubs as Clay before the war, became the Thunderbolt of the Confederacy; General Morgan and his men flashed into Lexington, raided the Bank of Kentucky for $10,000, and rode off with some $25,000 worth of Clay's horses from Ashland Stud. Kentucky, the colt, was in the north at the time; Clay had sent him to the races at Paterson, a new track across the river from New York City, where he won his only start in Clay's blue silks, as a two-year-old in the fall of 1863.

Kentucky was in the marvelous 1861 crop sired by Lexington. Not until Bull Lea sired Citation, Coaltown, and Bewitch in the same crop did a sire get in one year such a triumvirate as Norfolk, undefeated in five starts, Asteroid, undefeated in 12 starts, and Kentucky, beaten only by Norfolk. This defeat came in the inaugural Jersey Derby, $1,000-added at 1½ miles, run at Paterson on June 7, 1864. Norfolk won easily from Tipperary, Eagle was third, and Kentucky finished fourth in the field of twelve. Norfolk and Kentucky never met again. Norfolk was purchased from his breeder, Robert Alexander, just before the Jersey Derby by Theodore Winters, and was shipped to California, where he raced three more times as a four-year-old and became a foundation sire in the West. Kentucky remained in the East, where he was to win his next twenty races over three seasons to reign as unchallenged champion.

Kentucky raced in the colors of John Hunter, who thirty years later was to be elected first chairman of The Jockey Club, but he was owned in partnership with

161

William R. Travers and George Osgood. Two days after the Jersey Derby, Kentucky was brought back in the $300-added Sequel Stakes at two miles, won easily, and then was rested two months until the Saratoga meeting.

Saratoga had held its first meeting the previous year, with races run over the narrow Horse Haven track. In 1864 the wider track across Union Avenue was completed, and on the first day, August 2, the first race over the New Course was a new $1,000-added stakes at 1¾ miles, named in honor of the track president—Travers, who owned a third of the winner. Kentucky was ridden by the Bill Shoemaker of his day, Gilpatrick, who had won with Kentucky's sire, Lexington, in the 1850s, and with Lexington's sire, Boston, in the 1830s. Gilpatrick brought Kentucky down in the inaugural Travers Stakes by three lengths, beating Zeb Ward's Tipperary, Francis Morris's Throg's Neck Jr., and two others. Three days later, in the $500-added Sequel Stakes at two miles, Kentucky beat Tipperary and Throg's Neck Jr. again, in a field of four.

Shipped back to Paterson, Kentucky won the $1,000-added Jersey St. Leger at 2¼ miles on September 13. Two days after that, he won the $300-added Sequel Stakes, two miles in 3:50 carrying a seven-pound penalty for having won the Travers and Jersey St. Leger. He was fit and getting fitter.

His third race in four days at Paterson was at two-mile heats—a match race, $2,500 a side, against J. S. Watson's good older horse, Aldebarn. Kentucky won in convincing fashion, straight heats, the fastest two miles he ever raced: 3:47 in the first heat, and right back twenty minutes later in faster time, 3:40½ for the second heat. It does not happen now, a Travers winner racing 8¼ miles in four days in September, beating the best horses in the East—but it was the way Kentucky wound up his three-year-old season.

At four, Kentucky ran out of competition. From June through October he was unbeaten in seven races, four of these involving heats at two and three miles. He was allowed to walk over, without opposition in two races. Looking for a sporting proposition, Hunter and Travers issued a challenge to anybody, everybody, to race against Kentucky at $10,000 or $50,000 a side—no takers.

Meanwhile, Asteroid was beating everything in the Midwest. His breeder, Robert Alexander, always contended that Asteroid was better than Norfolk, which he had sold and sent to California for a dollar more than the record price he had paid for their great sire Lexington ($15,000), and nothing in St. Louis or Kentucky could catch the colt he had kept. There was speculation that Asteroid would be shipped East to meet Kentucky in the first running of the Saratoga Cup, but he did not appear. Kentucky easily won the $1,000-added Saratoga Cup, beating J. S. Watson's older Capt. Moore and Ward and McGrath's older Rhynodine by running the 2¼ miles in 4:01½

To offset suggestions that he feared Kentucky, Alexander proposed that Asteroid and Kentucky have a series of two match races for $10,000 a side, to be raced in Louisville. Hunter countered with a proposition that one match be run in New York, one in Kentucky. Proposals and counterproposals continued to appear in the sporting journals in the fall of 1865, but the season was over before a place and bet were arranged.

The next year, five-year-old Kentucky continued his string of victories through seven races. For Kentucky's first outing in June at Paterson, two-mile heats, Alexander tested the water, shipping up a four-year-old gelding by Lexington named Norwich. In the four-horse field Kentucky won, drawing away in the first heat, and "distanced" Alexander's horse in the second, that is, passed the finishing post before Norwich reached the distance pole, 100 yards back, in a two-mile heat race. So Alexander had a line on Kentucky and said no more about a match with Asteroid. Jerome

Park was to be completed by September, and a nice race was scheduled for the opener, $5,000-added The Inaugural Stakes. Alexander pointed Asteroid for that, and a showdown with Kentucky.

Meanwhile, Kentucky raced on, leaving all in his wake, day after day. On June 5 he started his season by beating Norwich at two-mile heats; on June 6 he won a three-mile dash race in 6:04¼; on June 7 he won at three-mile heats in faster time, 5:54¼ for the first, 5:19½ in the second heat. That amounted to thirteen miles of racing in three days; Kentucky then was given a six-week rest to prepare for Saratoga.

For almost a century, the Saratoga Cup served as the ultimate test of courage and stamina for the best horses in America. Kentucky won the first one in 1865 and the second in 1866, beating T. C. Moore's Beacon, Thomas Buford's Delaware, and J. W. Weldon's Leatherlungs. Four days later at Saratoga he won at four miles, in 7:31½, in preparation for Jerome Park's The Inaugural Stakes, to be run at four-mile heats. Alexander shipped Asteroid east for the long-awaited meeting with Kentucky. He was entered for The Inaugural, trained well for it at Jerome Park, but a week before the race he pulled up lame in a workout and was retired, undefeated. Kentucky had no difficulty winning The Inaugural in straight heats, 7:35 and 7:41½, defeating Leonard Jerome's Fleetwing, J. S. Watson's Onward, and Alexander's good mare by Lexington, Idlewild. Kentucky earned his richest prize, $6,900 and a silver cup valued at $1,500.

Jerome (Winston Churchill's grandfather) had selected and bought the site for his park, raised the money to build the track, named it after himself, and solicited 3,000 members for the club; then August Belmont I was elected president. And Jerome could not even win a race there. He talked to his friends Hunter and Travers about this state of affairs, and they finally agreed to sell Jerome Kentucky at an unprecedented price for a race horse—$40,000. A week after his track opened, Jerome won a race there, Kentucky winning the $1,000-added Grand National Handicap at 2¾ miles, giving nineteen to twenty-four pounds to old rivals Aldebarn, Nannie Butler, Onward, and Luther. So much the best was Kentucky that Jerome thought it a point of embarrassment for other owners to continue sending their horses down to defeat against him. He decided to retire Kentucky to stud, with a record of twenty-one victories in twenty-two starts, after the Grand National.

Following the 1867 breeding season, Kentucky acted as though he wanted to get back on the race track. There was no horse in the country capable of running with him, so Jerome thought about running him against time. His sire had set the world record for four miles at 7:19¾, and in a dozen years no horse had approached the mark. Jerome bet $5,000 that Kentucky could beat that time. After a year's absence, the six-year-old was brought back to Jerome Park on October 17, 1867, to race against the watch and the legend of his sire. Gilpatrick, who had ridden Lexington when he set the record in New Orleans, had not ridden Kentucky since he was a four-year-old; Charles Littlefield was his regular rider at five and had the mount against time.

Kentucky raced the first mile in 1:48, three-quarters of a second slower than Lexington's first mile; Littlefield sent him along at exactly the same pace for the second mile, and he picked up three seconds on Lexington's split for two miles. He ran three miles in 5:29 flat, two seconds faster than Lexington had run the same distance, carrying but 103 pounds, while Kentucky was carrying 120 pounds.

It matters not, the fractions in a race against time. One must go that last mile. Kentucky tired. Lexington had run that fourth mile in 1:48¾; Kentucky, his want

165

of racing condition revealed at last, could do no better than 2:02¾, for a final mark of 7:31¾—a dozen seconds slower than his sire's record.

Soon after Kentucky lost in his attempt to break Lexington's mark, the Annieswood Stable was formed by Jerome, Travers, Hunter, Belmont, and Sir Roderick Cameron; Kentucky was absorbed in this syndicate but never raced for Annieswood. A year later, the Annieswood Stable—which involved all the leading owners in New York, so who was there to race against?—was dispersed, and Kentucky was put up for auction. Belmont bought him for $15,000 to stand at his new Nursery Stud on Long Island.

Kentucky had a short stud career, dying in 1875, the same year as his sire. Among his best progeny was Woodbine, champion three-year-old filly of 1872, when she won the Alabama, Monmouth Oaks, and Hunter Stakes. That same year, his two-year-old daughter Medora beat Tom Bowling in the July Stakes, and his two-year-old colt Silk Stocking won the Kentucky Stakes. His best colt was Bertram, which won the 1876 Jersey Derby. Kentucky also sired stakes winners Beatrice, Count d'Orsay, Countess, and Carita, but none approached his class.

JOHN HENRY

JOHN HENRY was a steel-drivin' man. The legendary
Paul Bunyan of railroad construction crews, John
Henry was challenged more than a century ago by a
gang foreman with a new-fangled steam drill. At the
time, blasting bores were drilled into rock by steel-
driving men using long-handled, ten-pound sledge
hammers. John Henry did not fool around with ordinary sledges—he wielded twenty-pounders, one in
each mighty hand. The challenge is said to have been
made during the building of the C & O's Big Bend Tun-
nel in West Virginia. The whole crew got down bets, for
while the steam drill had awesome power, working men
would not believe any machine could beat a real steel-
drivin' man.

And the foreman turned on his steam machine, and
John Henry picked up his hammers. And lightning
from dark clouds started the contest, but thunder was
never heard; it was muted by the sound of John Henry's
hammers striking steel, reverberating through the
West Virginia hills. And they drilled, side by side, man
and machine, until the machine played out, on just one
hole, while John Henry had drilled *two* holes, each
seven feet deep, in solid rock. Some say John Henry
died then, when a blood vessel broke. Others say he
died later, when a mountain shuddered at his blows,

and tumbled down on him. Of such stuff, folk heroes are made. And folk songs sung.

Woodsong Farm owner John E. Callaway liked to name his yearlings after songs. At the 1976 Keeneland January sale, Callaway bought a newly turned yearling, by Ole Bob Bowers—Once Double, by Double Jay, from the consignment of his breeder, Mrs. Robert Lehmann's Golden Chance Farm near Paris, Kentucky. Callaway paid $1,100 for this colt, bought him for a song more or less, and named him for the folksong hero John Henry. Thus another legend began, with a legendary prologue, for John Henry, the $1,100 yearling with a throw-away pedigree, was to become the greatest money winner in the history of the Turf, the first to earn $6 million, voted the best race horse in America at the advanced age of nine.

"Actually, I bought him too cheap," Callaway said. "If I had paid more, I probably still would own him. I was ready to go to $5,000, because I liked his pedigree. I had been racing over at Ellis Park and kept getting beat by an Ole Bob Bowers colt, and I decided I better get one by Ole Bob Bowers. Then this little one came into the ring at Keeneland, out of a Double Jay mare, and I got him for only $1,100, I suppose because he was so small, and calf-kneed."

Then, too, Ole Bob Bowers yearlings had no great market demand, his fifteen sale yearlings averaging only $1,133 at the time. Two months before John Henry was sold, Ole Bob Bowers had been offered at Keeneland as a twelve-year-old stallion with two crops of racing age, and was auctioned for only $900.

Callaway turned out his little Ole Bob Bowers colt at Woodsong Farm near Louisville to let him grow.

"My veterinarian didn't like him," Callaway said. "He was small, and so back at the knees—he never seemed to be able to pick up his feet, kept stumbling all the time. He would stumble over a matchstick. And he was trouble in the stall, kept tearing up everything. My veterinarian kept telling me to get rid of him, and I didn't have much money in him. If I had bid more, say $5,000, why I would have figured I had too much money in him to dump him, and probably would have kept him. We never did try to break him to the saddle, just walked him around the shedrow, and put him back in the 1977 Keeneland January sale."

Young Harold Snowden, Jr., whose father is the managing partner of The Stallion Station near Lexington, was buying ten racing prospects to break, train, and sell. He bought John Henry as a newly turned two-year-old for $2,200 at Keeneland.

"Charlie Adams had won some races at Keeneland with Ole Bob Bowers colts, and I thought that might give me a reselling point," Snowden said. "I took him out to the farm to break him and found he was just terrible in the stall. He was all right outside the stall, but inside—he figured that was his domain, and he was the boss in there. He stripped his stall. Tore the feed tub from the wall, put his foot in the water bucket, tore up the webbing. But he was kind outside the stall, and we broke him easily, thirty or forty days on the farm, then sent him to Keeneland at the end of February. He kept tearing up his stall there, too, knocking the screen down, beating up buckets; we had to strap his feed tub to the wall down low; he really was a nuisance. So when my vet, Dr. Jim Boutcher, suggested he be gelded, we cut him, and that calmed him down some; we gave him a U-necked screen, and he liked that.

"He was coming along all right, galloping there at Keeneland, and I sold him for $7,500 to Akiko Mc-Varish, who gave me the check, but the sale was subject to her veterinarian's approval. Well, he wouldn't approve him—he was a little back at the knees, but he was sound and didn't have a pimple on him—so I had to give the money back and look for another buyer. Then Colleen Madere called me from Louisiana, asked if I had anything ready to run down there. Her trainer,

Phil Marino, came to Kentucky and galloped the horse himself, said he was all right, so I sold John Henry during the second week in May as a two-year-old for $10,000. Shipped him to Jefferson Downs and he won his first start."

John Henry won a small stakes at Evangeline Downs that fall, the $10,000-added Lafayette Futurity, but did not win again that winter, in $25,000 and $20,000 claiming races at Fair Grounds.

"They called me the next spring," Snowden said, "wondered if I would take him back, and I did; traded them a pair of two-year-olds, a colt named Pay the Way [which was to win nineteen races and earn $55,902] and a filly named Separation Gap [which was to win three races and earn $15,725], and got John Henry back as a three-year-old during the 1978 Keeneland spring meeting."

Snowden ran John Henry in his own colors in an allowance race at Keeneland, and he finished fourth. Then trainer Bobby Donato called Snowden from New York, said he had a new man interested in buying a horse, and Snowden sold John Henry for the third time in a year, this time to Dot and Sam Rubin's new Dotsam Stable for $25,000. Shipped to New York, he won his first start for his new owner, in a $25,000 claiming race. Ten days later he was tried for the first time on grass, in a $35,000 claiming race at Belmont Park, and he won by fourteen lengths. It was the last time John Henry was offered for sale.

Sam Rubin, a native New Yorker, was a horse player for many years before he bought his first horse.

"I was a traveling salesman—in toys and sporting goods. I'd be in Boston, say, and about noon I'd knock off. They all knew where to find me—at Suffolk Downs or Rockingham. In St. Louis I'd be at Cahokia Downs or Fairmount Park. I was a fellow who thought betting at the races was a way to wealth for someone who earned $20 a week," Rubin said. "Took me twenty-five years to learn. But I always was able to control myself. Whatever I lost, I lost; never borrowed money to bet. During those years, I developed as a handicapper; went from mediocre to poor."

For some twenty years, Rubin was a bicycle salesman for a Japanese firm. In 1973 he started his own company, importing bicycles made in Korea. The Sam Rubin Bicycle Corporation now has offices and showrooms on Fifth Ave., near the site of the old Madison Square Garden, where the first international six-day bicycle race was held in 1891 with high-wheelers.

In 1978 Rubin said to his wife Dorothy, "I'm just going to take $50,000 and blow it buying horses. When I blow it, I'm out of racing." That day he went to Aqueduct and . . . "I saw Joe Taub, the computer expert, and I said, 'Hey, Joe, know anybody that's got a couple of $25,000 horses for sale?' He said if he heard of any, he'd let me know." This sort of inquiry at a race track can bring *rocket* returns. No sooner had Mr. and Mrs. Rubin been seated in the dining room than an agent stopped by the table, advised them of a nice $25,000 horse in Kentucky, and put Rubin in touch with Snowden. John Henry was bought over the telephone.

It is true that Rubin did not know John Henry was a gelding when he bought him, but his oft-quoted "What color is a gelding?" was asked with a laugh, a piece of his self-deprecating humor. On the road, Rubin had learned much about horse racing, horses, and people. There are no naive horse players. He knew about winning and losing, and how mischance can change one to the other. He knew what a $25,000 three-year-old was, what a champion was, and what the chances were of one developing into the other. And the chances of his owning such a champion?

"Incredible, blind, luck," he said after John Henry won the Arlington Million the first time. "I just happened to make a phone call at the right time." Rubin brought to racing an understanding and appreciation of the game that few owners acquire in years.

After winning his first two starts in claiming races for Rubin, John Henry won an allowance race, then placed in three stakes, won another allowance race at Belmont in September 1978, and was shipped to Chicago. Bobby Donato sent him out for the $50,000-added Round Table Handicap, and John Henry came back a winner by twelve lengths. Shipped to California for a week, he finished third and sixth in stakes at Oak Tree, then was flown back to Penn National and won a division of the $20,000-added Chocolatetown Handicap.

"We got a trophy and a great big box of chocolate kisses," Rubin recalled of the first time he saw John Henry win a stakes for him. "I don't think my feet touched the ground. I ate all those kisses myself."

That was the end of John Henry's three-year-old season. He was shipped to Ocala and turned out. For Rubin and Donato he had won six races, five of them on grass, two of these stakes. He had shown enough for F. E. Kilroe to rank him among the ten top three-year-olds at 120 pounds on *The Blood-Horse* Free Handicap (equal weight with Joe Taub's Sensitive Prince). Kilroe put Triple Crown winner Affirmed at the top with 133 pounds, one more than Alydar. Champion grass horse Mac Diarmida was ranked third with 130 pounds; and John Henry was the next-highest ranked three-year-old grass specialist.

In the spring of his four-year-old year John Henry was shipped from Florida to New York and placed in the care of trainer V. J. (Lefty) Nickerson.

"I was told he was tough," Nickerson said, "but he came to me very docile, easy to handle. I took him down to Monmouth Park, ran him on dirt in an allowance race, and he won by fourteen lengths. Se we took him up to Suffolk Downs for the Massachusetts Handicap, and he finished nowhere; we put him back on grass." He finished second in two turf stakes, won from wire to wire at Saratoga, came right back at Belmont, and won again on the lead.

"Waya, the champion grass mare, was third to him in that race, and that was the signal of what kind of horse John Henry was developing into," Nickerson said. In October 1979 there seemed to be little opportunity for John Henry on grass in New York, and Nickerson recommended that the four-year-old be shipped to California for the winter.

"I've got a good friend out there I grew up with, Ron McAnally, and he can take him." He did. John Henry arrived at 2 A.M. and McAnally saddled him for the $75,000-added Carleton F. Burke Handicap that afternoon; he finished second. Three weeks later he won a division of the $40,000-added Henry P. Russell Handicap.

The one stakes victory at four did not impress Kilroe. He weighted him low, at 116 pounds on *The Blood-Horse* Free Handicap, ten pounds below grass champion Bowl Game, eighteen below top-weighted Affirmed.

In 1980, at five, John Henry emerged as a champion on grass. On January 1, Darrel McHargue brought him down by a head in the San Gabriel. Three weeks later the San Marcos was taken off the grass because of rain, and John Henry won it anyway. He was flown across the country to Florida, picked up the Hialeah Turf Cup, and went back to California to win the 1½-mile San Luis Rey in 2:23 flat, equaling Santa Anita's record for the downhill course. Next he won the 1¾-mile San Juan Capistrano Invitational, and on May 26 made it six-for-six on the year, winning the 1½-mile Hollywood Invitational. McAnally sent him back to Nickerson in New York.

After finishing second twice, John Henry won the

Brighton Beach, ridden by Angel Cordero, Jr. (Mc-Hargue was on the ground with a seven-day suspension). John Henry then was tried on dirt again and finished second to champion three-year-old Temperence Hill in the Jockey Club Gold Cup.

He seemed to have tailed off in October, when he finished a distant third in the Turf Classic, but three weeks later in California he turned in his best race of the year in the Oak Tree Invitational. John Henry likes to make the pace, or race along just behind it. But Bill Shoemaker sent South African Bold Tropic to the early lead, and he was rating kindly with a three-length lead going by the stands the first time. John Henry was unusually far back, in the second flight; after a mile, he was six lengths back, and on the last turn Laffit Pincay stood up in his irons to avoid running up on the heels of another horse. John Henry dropped back to seventh place, eight lengths behind Bold Tropic.

"He was hit twice," Rubin noticed, "and he still came from far out of it. I never saw such determination. After we had given up, we were just hoping he'd pull up sound, there he came." He won, going away, by 1½ lengths.

Voted his first Eclipse Award as champion grass horse, John Henry was ranked by Kilroe on *The Blood-Horse* Free Handicap at 128 pounds, eight below Horse of the Year Spectacular Bid, one above grass specialist Tiller.

Better was John Henry at six: Horse of the Year, champion on grass, champion older horse on dirt or grass or gravel path, he was voted three Eclipse Awards. Another went to his owner, another to his trainer, another to his breeder, and his rider received two. He began by winning the San Luis Obispo, then took the Santa Anita Handicap on dirt. Back on grass, he won the San Luis Rey again, the Hollywood Invitational again. Rubin was on hand for all of these. On the day of the Hollywood Gold Cup in June 1981, Rubin's niece was getting married and he did not get to the track; John Henry lost.

"McAnally told me, 'No more weddings on weekends.'"

Shipped to Nickerson in New York, John Henry won the Sword Dancer in July, with Bill Shoemaker replacing Pincay. Shipped back to Del Mar to rest in August, he was then flown to Chicago for the first Arlington Million. John Henry can run on any kind of surface, but he does not care for deep sandy tracks (as for the Massachusetts Handicap) or soggy grass courses (as for the Arlington Million).

"He's a professional," Shoemaker said. "He just does the very best he can, all the time, gives you everything he has; no matter what the problem is, he goes to work. He did not like this deep going, and it took him a long time to get adjusted to it, you know, to get into his rhythm."

John Henry was eighth going by the stands the first time in the Arlington Million, four horses wide on the clubhouse turn. Shoemaker dropped John Henry down on the rail going down the backstretch in eighth place. Then he began to pick up horses. Coming out of the last turn, John Henry swung wide and took aim on the leader, The Bart.

"I knew I had enough horse," Shoemaker said later, "I just hoped I had enough ground. At the eighth pole, I saw Eddie Delahoussaye had a lot of horse left, and I knew it was going to take everything my little horse had."

Ole John Henry and ole Bill Shoemaker got that Million, at the very last moment, by the shortest of margins, a nose. In going he did not like, John Henry equaled the course record. It was his finest performance. It assured him another grass championship, and he was flown back to California.

Yet there was another challenge, for Horse of the

175

Year. In the East, Pleasant Colony had won the Kentucky Derby and Preakness, had beaten older horses in the Woodward, and had given weight when beaten in the Marlboro Cup. McAnally was not keen on the idea of loading up the old gelding for another trip across the country. He had the money and already had one championship. It was Rubin who made the decision to go for all of it, on the dirt, in the 1½-mile Jockey Club Gold Cup. John Henry turned back the challenge of Peat Moss, and Shoemaker brought him home by a head to win Horse of the Year honors.

Returned to California, John Henry won the Oak Tree Invitational again, by a neck, for his seventh triumph in eight races at six years. He was asked to run one more time, in December 1981, to pass the $3 million mark in earnings. He did that with fourth money in the Hollywood Turf Cup. Providential, fresh from victory in the Washington, D.C., International, ran by ole John and beat him by two lengths at level weight. Kilroe assigned John Henry topweight of 129 pounds on *The Blood-Horse* Free Handicap, only one pound above Providential, two above Flying Paster and Spence Bay.

In 1982, at seven, John Henry started in March, carrying 130 pounds in the Santa Anita Handicap. In a long drive he was beaten by a nose by Perrault (in receipt of four pounds), but was given his second victory in California's biggest race by the stewards, who disqualified Perrault. Just for that, Perrault beat him at level weights three weeks later in the San Luis Rey. John Henry wrenched his right front ankle in this race, and he was taken out of training for the first time since he was a three-year-old. Dr. Jack Robbins said there was no chance he could race by summer, and only a 60–40 chance the seven-year-old ever would race again.

McAnally brought him back slowly with love and care. In October John Henry was assigned 129 pounds for the Carleton F. Burke Handicap, and Mehmet, getting 12 pounds, beat him by 1½ lengths. Two weeks later John Henry won his third Oak Tree Invitational. It was too late in the year to come up with another Eclipse Award, but John Henry was feeling spry, and he was sent east for the Meadowlands Cup; he finished third to Mehmet, giving the winner eleven pounds.

Two weeks later he was in Tokyo, responding to the invitation he could not accept the previous year to run in the Japan Cup. Rubin was eager to run his horse before his business associates of many years, but John Henry inexplicably turned in his worst performance since the 1979 Massachusetts Handicap and finished thirteenth.

It was not a good year for John Henry, two wins in six starts, but earnings of $580,300 hardly could be called a bad year. Kilroe ranked him second high on *The Blood-Horse* Free Handicap with 126 pounds, two below grass champion Perrault, one above handicap champion Lemhi Gold.

Champion again at eight, John Henry was out until half the season was gone. On July 4, 1983, he won the American Handicap with Chris McCarron up, then was saved for the Budweiser Million eight weeks later, when an imported three-year-old, Tolomeo, beat him by a neck. Six weeks later, in New York for the Jockey Club Gold Cup, he turned in an uncharacteristically dull race, finishing fifth to champion three-year-old Slew o' Gold, and was returned to California. Seeking his fourth Oak Tree Invitational, he was second by a half-length to a four-year-old French filly, Zalataia.

About that time, the thought came that John Henry had lost his competitive fire, but in December of his eight-year-old season he won the rich Hollywood Turf

Cup. John Henry relaxed in second place behind a slow pace, tracked by Zalataia. The grand mare Sangue surged to the lead earlier than usual, as Prince Florimund faded, and John Henry "stopped running for me," McCarron said later. "There were a couple of soft spots coming around the turn, and he stepped in them. But once we got into the stretch, he seemed to sense the ground was firmer, and he got going again." In the last furlong, John Henry caught Sangue, but then on the outside Zalataia got her head in front at the sixteenth pole. She hung; John Henry kept on. He won again, for the thirty-third time. The $275,000 purse put him over the $4 million mark. No other horse had ever earned $3 million. And he won another Eclipse Award, champion grass horse at eight. Kilroe gave him 128 pounds on *The Blood-Horse* Free Handicap, two pounds above champion handicapper Bates Motel.

In 1984, John Henry was brought back to race again as a nine-year-old. No champion in the history of the American Turf raced so long, so well. Before the Civil War, mighty Boston won thirty-six of thirty-seven races to reign as undisputed champion from three years through eight; then a younger filly, Fashion, beat Boston in his last race at eight, and she trounced him at nine. Perennial handicap champion Kingston won stakes at two years through eight in the 1880s and 1890s, but could not handle stakes competition at nine and ten years. In this century, Old Rosebud, Exterminator, Grey Lag, and Armed, each champion in his youth, continued to win ordinary races at nine, but could not win stakes at that age. Five-time champion Kelso was unplaced in his only start at nine. Four-time champion Forego, and aged champions Stymie, Roseben, and Roamer stopped racing at eight.

Yet at nine, John Henry had his richest and most glorious season. He was voted champion grass horse for the fourth time, and for the second time was voted the best race horse in America, irrespective of racing surface, sex, or age. George Blanda, Bobby Hull, and Carl Yastrzemski, counted athletic marvels for retaining physical skills to compete on the highest level of professional sports many years after their original teammates had retired, provided no reference points for John Henry's sustained excellence. Like old wine, John Henry . . .

For his first start as a nine-year-old, John Henry was pointed for the Santa Anita Handicap. No other horse had ever won this fixture twice, and for John Henry's attempt to win it a third time, he was assigned top weight of 127 pounds. He stumbled at the start and was never in contention, finishing fifth, beaten eight lengths by four-year-old Interco, which was in receipt of six pounds.

Four weeks later, he was sent out on grass in the 1½-mile San Luis Rey, carrying equal weight of 126 pounds with Interco and Gato Del Sol, the latter winner of the Kentucky Derby two years earlier. John Henry got to the lead after a mile, but weakened and was passed by both Interco and Gato Del Sol in the stretch run, finishing third by three-quarters of a length. It seemed at that point that age finally had caught up with John Henry, and had passed him. This was not the case, however, for John Henry was to win five of his next six starts; with age, John Henry needed just a little more time into the season to find his best form.

Shipped from Los Angeles to San Francisco in May, John Henry was assigned top weight of 125 pounds for the Golden Gate Fields Handicap, 1⅜ miles on grass, and he broke the course record, winning in 2:13 by two lengths from ordinary horses. Three weeks later, he returned to Los Angeles to run in the 1½-mile Hollywood Invitational Turf Handicap, which he had won as a five-year-old in 2:25⅖, and had won as a six-year-old in 2:27⅘. As a nine-year-old, John Henry won his third Hollywood Invitational in stakes-record time of 2:25

flat, suggesting that he was even better than he had been when he was four years younger.

Then he was tried on dirt again, in the 1¼-mile Hollywood Gold Cup, and he was not able to handle the surface as he had in previous years. He lacked the acceleration he could demonstrate on grass, running evenly, two lengths behind the pacesetter most of the way; in the stretch run he did not pick up a yard of ground, and finished second by two lengths to Desert Wine. The latter could have picked up a million-dollar bonus by beating John Henry four weeks later in the Sunset Handicap, but that race was scheduled at 1½-miles on grass, and Desert Wine's owner and trainer did not feel their four-year-old could handle ole John Henry at that distance, on his turf, and did not even enter Desert Wine in the Sunset. John Henry won the Sunset easily, and then was pointed for the Budweiser-Arlington Million in Chicago.

He had won this million-dollar race the first time it was run in 1981, beating The Bart by a nose in a dramatic finish, and he had finished second in this race in 1983, beaten a neck by Tolomeo. When he returned in 1984, he drew a crowd three times Arlington Park's usual attendance; his fans came to see if John Henry could do it one more time.

"The others have youth," said his trainer, Ron McAnally, "but old John Henry has experience, and he still has phenomenal action. When he sees a hole, he'll go for it on his own. I don't believe the rider guided him off the rail at the head of the stretch; old John saw that opening and went for it."

John Henry had been running smoothly on grass he liked, saving ground along the rail, some two lengths behind pace-setting Royal Heroine, a champion four-year-old filly, and Nijinsky's Secret, a six-year-old grass specialist. On the last turn, Nijinsky's Secret began to drift wide, ever so slightly, and the old campaigner charged between the two younger horses. Nijinsky's

Secret immediately faded, Chris McCarron hit John Henry once, and he drove by the filly to win with power to spare, Royal Heroine finishing second by nearly two lengths and Gato Del Sol getting up late for third. First money of $600,000 pushed John Henry's career earnings over the $5 million mark.

Los Angeles in July—Chicago in August—John Henry was in New York in September for the rich Turf Classic and a meeting with All Along, a five-year-old French mare. The previous season, All Along had won the Prix de l'Arc de Triomphe in Paris, the Rothmans International in Toronto, the Turf Classic in New York, and the Washington, D.C., International in Maryland—all within six weeks—and was voted Horse of the Year in America. Although All Along was making only her first start in eleven months, her French trainer said she was ready, as good as she had been the previous fall. He was wrong. John Henry took the lead at the onset, which was not his usual style, then set a relatively slow early pace; he ran the first half-mile in :48⅘, which permitted him to run the second half-mile faster, in :48⅖, and the final half-mile even faster, in :48 flat. All Along never got closer than fourth. John Henry was challenged in the stretch by a horse with the name for it, but Win could not get by, and John Henry beat Win by a neck in 2:25⅕, stakes record time. First money in the Turf Classic raised John Henry's career earnings to $5,851,860.

Before the Turf Classic, management at Meadowlands announced that it would raise the value of its Ballantine Scotch Classic Handicap from $200,000 (first money in that purse would not have been enough to put John Henry over the $6 million mark) to $400,000 guaranteed, and a $500,000 bonus would be awarded to the winner of both the Turf Classic and The Ballantine Scotch Classic. To attract the owner of racing's biggest superstar, the money was right, and the weight was right—126 pounds. Rubin had let it be known that he did not believe a nine-year-old should be expected to carry more than 126 pounds; consequently, track handicappers hoping to have John Henry run at their tracks thought it best to fix the topweight at 126, and scale his competition down from there.

In the usual order of things, a handicap horse is assigned higher weight after winning a handicap race, while other horses in the beaten field are assigned lower weights for the next encounter, the idea being to handicap the better horses with high weight, the lesser horses with low weight, and by such handicapping, to bring all horses together in a competitive finish. Under this traditional system, John Henry would be required to carry successively higher weights with each victory. But his owner would not have elected to run John Henry with higher weight, so to get John Henry as a gate attraction, he was assigned 126 pounds again, and Meadowlands, whose attendance averaged some 14,000, drew a crowd of 37,112 to see John Henry race.

Coming from eighth place in a field of twelve, ole John Henry rushed by younger rivals to assume command in the stretch, and pulled away to win by almost three lengths, equalling the course record for 1⅜ miles in 2:13 flat. In his last race of 1984, the purse and bonus amounted to $740,000, richest prize in John Henry's long career, and raised his lifetime earnings to $6,591,860. In eighty-two races, he finished first thirty-nine times, second fifteen times, and third nine times through eight racing seasons.

At this writing the three greatest money earners in the history of the Turf are John Henry with $6,591,860; Slew o' Gold with $3,533,534; and All Along with $3,018,420. Five other horses that raced in North America have earned more than $2 million each in purses. In all, sixty-two horses have earned more than a million dollars each in purses since 1951, when Citation became the first equine millionaire. Because of inflation, it is difficult to place in perspective the relation of earnings to racing merit of a Thoroughbred. Factoring out inflation by converting current dollars to 1967 constant dollars, the list of leading money winners of the Turf is still topped by John Henry.

With actual earnings in current dollars converted to 1967 constant dollars, the ten leading earners would be: (1) John Henry (foaled in 1975) with $2,353,826; (2) Kelso (foaled in 1957) with $2,175,501; (3) Round Table (foaled in 1954) with $2,041,131; (4) Nashua (foaled in 1952) with $1,599,486; (5) Stymie (foaled in 1941) with $1,554,152; (6) Buckpasser (foaled in 1963) with $1,514,352; (7) Citation (foaled in 1945) with $1,507,741; (8) Carry Back (foaled in 1958) with $1,405,063; (9) Armed (foaled in 1941) with $1,359,470; and (10) Spectacular Bid (foaled in 1976) with $1,238,150. Recent $3 million earners Slew o' Gold and All Along rank sixteenth and twenty-sixth when actual earnings in current dollars are converted to 1967 constant dollars.

Voted champion grass horse, and Horse of the Year over Slew o' Gold as a nine-year-old, John Henry could not be expected to improve as a ten-year-old. But, then, no one expected him to be better at nine than at eight. Whether he ever races again—and at this writing, his racing future is unknown—it matters not, for the legend of John Henry will live on for many years. John Henry was the backward yearling with an unfashionable pedigree that was sold as a yearling for $1,100, that ran on, and on, and on, to riches and everlasting fame.

Index

Note: Italic numbers indicate illustrations

chairman, New York Racing Commission, Jockey Club, 117; purchased and rebuilt Saratoga Race Course, builder of Belmont Park, Beldame first great horse bred by, 118; auctions yearlings, sells Man o' War, 120

Belmont, August, II: breeder of 129 stakes winners, 36

Belmont Park, 116, 118

Belmont Stakes: Calumet Farm winners of, 42; John E. Madden breeder of five winners of, 111

Ben Brush: 1896 Kentucky Derby winner, 160

Bennington, Newton: leases Beldame, 118

Berryman, Charley: president, Raceland, 8

Bertram: Kentucky sire of, 166

Bewitch: first filly to earn $460,000, 44

Big Red. See Man o' War

Blaze: first English stallion imported to Kentucky, 17

Blenheim II: sire of 530 foals, 72; purchased by Arthur B. Hancock, Sr., sire of Whirlaway, 138

Bluegrass region of Kentucky, 13

Bold Lad: champion 2-year-old in England, 1966, 140

Bold Ruler, 145; voted best race horse in America in 1957, leader on general sire list eight times, 131; foaled at Claiborne Farm, 132; Nasrullah sire of, 144; racing record, 146–49; last race of, career as sire, 149; leading sire, 150; death of in 1971, sire of Secretariat, 152

Boone, Daniel: brought horses into Kentucky, 13

Boston: sire of Lexington, 24

Boundless: 1893 American Derby winner, 1

Bradford, John: began first newspaper west of Alleghenies, 14

Bradley, Colonel E. R.: successful Thoroughbred breeder, 36

Breckinridge, John C.: president, Kentucky Association race track, purchased Cabell's Dale (Castleton) farm in 1790, 67

Breckinridge, Robert J. (son of John): breeder of Thoroughbreds, president of Centre College, daughter married John Castleton, 67

Breeders' Cup: provided $10 million in purses in 1984, 97

Breeders Sales Company, 139

breeding: of mares smaller than 14 hands prohibited by Henry VIII, 33; challenge of time, 34; challenge of probabilities and money, 35

Broeck, Richard Ten: owner of Metairie Course, heads syndicate that acquired Lexington, 25; acquires full ownership of Lexington, 28; retires Lexington to stud duty at Nantura Stud, sells Lexington to R. A. Alexander, 30

Brown, Ed (Brown Dick): sells Plaudit to John E. Madden, 100

Brown, Henry (Burbridge's Harry): trainer of Lexington, 24

Bruce, Colonel Sanders B.: compiles first volume of *American Stud Book*, 20; Jockey Club acquires *American Stud Book*, 56, 117

Buford, General Abe: buyer of

185

1913, 110; development of
subway system in, 114–15
New York Racing Commission:
August Belmont II chairman
of, 93; established in 1895,
117
Nickerson, V. J. (Lefty):
trainer of John Henry, 172
Noor: wins over Citation, 53
Norfolk: champion sired by
Lexington, 32; defeats Ken-
tucky, sold and shipped to
California, becomes sire, 161
Northern Dancer: yearling colt
sired by auctioned, 56
Nursery Stud: August Belmont
II breeder of 129 stakes win-
ners at, 36; Man o' War
foaled at, 112; established in
New York by August Bel-
mont, Sr., moved to Ken-
tucky, 116

Oaklands: Henry Clay frequent
visitor to, 158
Old Rosebud: 1914 Kentucky
Derby winner, John E. Mad-
den breeder of, 111
Old Rowley: ridden to victory
by Charles II, 33
Ole Bob Bowers: sire of John
Henry, 168
Once Double: dam of John
Henry, 168
Orby: wins 1907 English
Derby, 70

Papyrus: defeated by Zev in
1923, 33
pari-mutuel wagering: tax revenues generated by, 55
Parole: best handicapper in
1878, 64
Patrick, Gilbert Watson (Gil-
patrick): rides Lexington to
victory in world-record time,
30

Paul Jones: 1920 Kentucky
Derby winner, John E. Madden breeder of, 111
Pensive: Kentucky Derby winner in 1944, 42
Phipps, Gladys Livingston
Mills (Mrs. Henry C.): mar-
ries, 139; death of, 141; with
Bold Ruler, 145
Phipps, Henry Carnegie:
founder of United States
Steel, marries, 139; estab-
lishes Wheatley Stable, 140,
death of, 141
Phoenix Hotel Stakes: original
name of Association Stakes,
first race for Lexington
(horse), 24
Pilgarlick: pedigree of adver-
tised in newspaper, 14
Plaudit: defeats Ben Brush, 96;
bought by John E. Madden,
racing record of, sold to
W. C. Whitney, 100
Poa pratensis, 13
Polk, James: defeats Henry
Clay in election, 159
Ponder: Kentucky Derby win-
ner in 1949, 42
Preakness Stakes: Calumet
Farm winner of, seven
times, 42
Princequillo: sire at Claiborne
Farm, 142; as leading sire,
143
Prince Simon: sired by Prince-
quillo, champion in England,
143
Princess Doreen: John E.
Madden breeder of, 111
Pryor, John B.: trainer of Lex-
ington, 26
purses: exceed $547 million in
1983, 55; richest of, 97

Raceland: race track at Ashland, 6; 1926 meeting of, 9
Raceland Derby, 1

193